holding *His* hand
a devotional for teen girls

holding *His* hand
a devotional for teen girls
beka dewitt

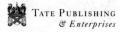
TATE PUBLISHING
& Enterprises

Tate Publishing is committed to excellence in the publishing industry. Our staff of highly trained professionals, including editors, graphic designers, and marketing personnel, work together to produce the very finest books available. The company reflects the philosophy established by the founders, based on Psalms 68:11,

"THE LORD GAVE THE WORD AND GREAT WAS THE COMPANY OF THOSE WHO PUBLISHED IT."

If you would like further information, please contact us:
1.888.361.9473 | www.tatepublishing.com
TATE PUBLISHING & Enterprises, LLC | 127 E. Trade Center Terrace
Mustang, Oklahoma 73064 USA

Holding His Hand: A Devotional for Teen Girls

Scripture quotations marked "KJV" are taken from the Holy Bible, King James Version, Cambridge, 1769. Used by permission. All rights reserved.

Cover design by Melanie Harr-Hughes
Interior design by Janae Glass

Published in the United States of America

ISBN: 1-5988697-4-4

06.11.30

To my mother,
whose selfless love and godly example
guided me through not only my teen years
but my every day.

I have had the privilege of watching Beka DeWitt grow up to the mature, godly young lady that she is today. Beka was a part of the teen class led by my husband. She faithfully participated with a servant's heart, always willing and wanting to do for others. And now, though just a young woman, she has a deep interest in helping teenage girls.

The lessons provided in *Holding His Hand* challenge the reader to draw closer to God, to be better than she is, and to set and reach goals that she possibly would not otherwise have reached. Read this devotional with anticipation of what God can do for you through His precious truths and practical lessons as they seep into your mind and heart.

It is my belief that if the hearts of young ladies can be captured while in their teen years, not only by someone who really cares, but by the truths that emit from the Word of God, these young ladies will have a better chance of one day becoming godly wives and mothers.

Diana Williams

I closed my eyes and squeezed my hand tighter. My hand hung at my side, cupped as if holding another hand. I silently prayed, asking for courage and strength to get through the day. God's peace surrounded me as I walked on—my hand in His.

This book has been birthed from the moments I've joined hands with God whether it be five minutes before my history of civilization exam or the day I found out my mother had cancer. In these moments, God has taught me numerous valuable truths. I pray I can share these truths with you in a way that will make you yearn to be closer to God. To know that He is *always* beside you, comforting you, loving you, and bearing your load. And anytime you need Him to, He'll hold *your* hand.

Lying on the sidewalk only an inch from an ant, he said, "Hi, I'm Sam." The four-year-old I baby-sit was trying to converse with an ant. He peered intently at the ant, as if waiting for a reply. I tried to explain.

"Sam, ants don't talk like people do. It's just like how dogs and people can't understand each other. People talk and dogs bark."

He hesitated, "Bark. Bark."

Just like Sam was trying so hard to communicate to an ant, God desperately wants to communicate with his children. Most of the time our excuses are "I'm too busy!" or "I'm too tired!" or even "I don't feel like it!" But the only way we can hear God speaking to us is when we make the time and effort to read His loving words.

It would be awful if you couldn't catch up with your best friend on all the happenings of the day when you were out of school sick. You would be upset having missed all the stories of what went on that day. It's the same way with God. He's sad when we don't take the time to hear from Him. And His Word is a lot more important than the school gossip. Don't make it hard for God to communicate with you. He has so *much* to tell you.

Just Wait!

Do you get aggravated or even depressed when one of your friends announces that she is now officially dating? Do you become jealous instead of happy for a friend when you see her with her boyfriend? Do you often comment, "I'll never get asked out," or "I'll never get married," or "Guys are dumb," just to hide your true feelings of loneliness?

If you replied "yes" to any of these questions, don't feel bad. There are *many* girls going through the exact same thing. It *is* hard to sit home on Friday night when all of your friends have dates! It *is* hard to watch almost every girl in school get something for Valentine's Day, and yet, you haven't received a Valentine card in three years. So what are you supposed to do? Join a convent? Become easy? Date the nerds? Or course not! God says to *wait*.

Isaiah 40:31 says, "But they that wait upon the Lord shall renew their strength; they shall mount up with wings as eagles; they shall run, and not be weary; and they shall walk, and not faint." God will give you the strength to wait for the right person. And when you do meet that special someone, you'll be happy you waited. God is preparing a spouse for you right now. To fit you in every way. To complete you. To be your best friend.

God knows the perfect time to orchestrate the crossing of your paths. You just have to trust Him. (Proverbs 3:5-6) Because God knows everything, He knows what's best for you. And while you're waiting, try praying for your future spouse. Pray that he'll have patience and reliance on God while he is also waiting. Or make a list of important characteristics that you are looking for in a spouse. (Be reasonable!) And try to stick to your list when you do bump into a guy who makes your heart dance so you won't just settle on dating any average Joe. Make sure it is someone who has been worth the wait.

Lastly, don't lose hope. Jacob had to work *fourteen* years before he could marry the woman he loved! But he got her in the end. Trust God while you wait. And you never know, maybe tomorrow you'll meet that special someone.

If you were to ask your friends to name five characteristics about you, what do you think they would say? Maybe that you're humble? Funny? Serious? Selfish? Optimistic? Boy crazy? There are many ways to describe someone—good and bad. Knowing a few characteristics about someone would give a person a good idea about what he would be like.

So what about the characteristics of God? Could you name a few? In Hebrews 13:8, it says, "Jesus Christ the same yesterday, and today, and forever." In this passage, we see that God is *eternal*. He has always been, and He will always be.

God is also *omnipresent*, meaning He is everywhere at the same time. Matthew 28:20b shows this when Jesus says, "Lo, I am with you always, even unto the end of the world. Amen."

God is also all-knowing or *omniscient*. He knows what each of us is thinking all the time. (Luke 6:8a)

In Matthew 8:27, we see that God is *omnipotent* or all-powerful. In this verse, men are marveling that even the wind and the sea obey Jesus. All of Jesus' miracles prove that He is all-powerful.

God is also *immutable*. He doesn't change. We *never* have to worry about God changing His mind. (Hebrews 1:12)

All of these attributes help us to see who God really is. It is comforting to know that we have a God who is eternal, omnipresent, omniscient, omnipotent, and immutable! Thank God today for who He is!

Scripture of the Day: John 1:1–4

Dear Lord,

I ask vengeance on serial killers, rapists, and terrorists. Consume them with your fiery anger, Lord. (Psalm 59:13) Break their teeth out from their mouths. (Psalm 58:6) Shoot them with Your arrows, for they are wicked. (Psalm 64:7) Make them to know that You alone are God. Judge them, Lord, as thou wilt.

Amen

Did you know that this prayer is called an imprecatory prayer? Imprecatory prayers are those that ask God for judgment and vengeance on the deserving person. I never would have thought that praying evil upon someone would be allowed in God's eyes. But David prayed numerous times for judgment on his enemies. That's the important thing; when someone does evil against us, it's not up to us to put "our enemy" in his place. It's up to God to judge him.

Romans 12:19 says, "Dearly beloved, avenge not yourselves, but rather give place unto wrath: for it is written, Vengeance is mine; I will repay, saith the Lord." Let God take care of all those who have wronged you. He will "tread down our enemies" much better than we could ever imagine. (Psalm 60:12) In the meantime, pray an imprecatory prayer against God's enemies.

15

The following are actual statements found on insurance forms where car drivers attempted to summarize the details of an accident.[1]

- Coming home I drove into the wrong house and collided with a tree I don't have.
- The other car collided with mine without giving warning of its intentions.
- I thought my window was down, but I found it was up when I put my head through it.
- I collided with a stationary truck coming the other way.
- A truck backed through my windshield into my wife's face.
- The guy was all over the road. I had to swerve a number of times before I hit him.
- I pulled away from the side of the road, glanced at my mother-in-law and headed over the embankment.
- In an attempt to kill a fly, I drove into a telephone pole.
- I had been shopping for plants all day and was on my way home. As I reached an intersection a hedge sprang up, obscuring my vision and I did not see the other car.
- I had been driving for forty years when I fell asleep at the wheel and had an accident.

Although these excuses are quite humorous, it is hard to believe that people actually used them as reasons for car accidents. You have to wonder what they were thinking at the time! But we can't judge them because so often we make the same lousy excuses. (Romans 2:1-16) Excuses why we can't wash the dishes, go to church on Sunday nights, witness to our friends, and so on. We blame it on time, friends, responsibilities, shyness, and even our rights. Yet all of our excuses remain futile before God. It's not *why* we didn't do something, but *if* we did it that matters.

Moses tried four times to justify why he couldn't lead the children of Israel out of Egypt. He gave excuses like: "Who am I, that I should go unto Pharaoh?"; "They will not believe me"; and "I am not eloquent." However, none of Moses' excuses succeeded in getting him out of the job God had for him. Every time Moses threw out an excuse, God responded, showing him why his excuse wasn't valid. God had a job for Moses. And God equipped him so that he *could* get the job done.

It's the same way in our lives. God has certain tasks and responsibilities for each one of us. He doesn't want to hear our excuses. He wants to hear us say, "Yes, Lord."

I had just finished writing a personal essay for my college writing class. I had poured my heart out onto the paper, literally shedding sweat and tears. Still, I felt so unconfident. Our teacher told us to divide up into groups of three or four and read our papers aloud for critiquing.

Heart pounding and hands shaking, I read page after page of my paper. I wondered how my classmates were going to react. After all, I was sharing some of my innermost hopes and dreams. What if they thought my paper was stupid? How would I handle it? I finally finished and waited anxiously to hear their remarks.

In the end, I received some good comments and some bad. But the thing I remember most about this incident was the note I later received from Tracy, a member of my group. She wrote, "I just wanted to let you know how much I enjoyed your paper. I *really* did. It was so personal, yet so relatable…." I couldn't stop smiling after I read her note. It made my day.

Sometimes, we don't realize how far an act of kindness can really go—whether it is a note, a smile, a hug, or a box of chocolates. We would all love to receive any of these, especially on a bad day. And as the saying goes, "Do unto others as you would have them do unto you." We should try *everyday* to do something kind for others.

You might never know just how much an act of kindness can mean to someone. I'm sure Tracy has no idea that a year later, I still have her note hanging on my bulletin board.

Drop a word of cheer and kindness:
just a flash and it is gone;
But there's half-a-hundred ripples
circling on and on,
Bearing hope and joy and comfort on
each splashing, dashing wave.
Till you wouldn't believe the volume
of the one kind word you gave.

-James W. Foley[2]

The Pimple Prayer

When you were a child, how long did your Christmas and birthday lists end up measuring? A foot long? Three feet long? Ten feet long? I'm sure our parents were relieved when these holidays finally passed so they didn't have to hear us whine, "Mommy, can I please have it?" or "Daddy, I want that really bad!" anymore. We would beg them morning, noon, and night for our desired toys, whether for Barbie's dream house or a pink and purple bike.

But even though the years have changed our desires (I hope!), we should still be begging our Heavenly Father to answer our prayer needs. Jesus longs to hear our every request no matter how insignificant it may seem. If you're hoping for that monstrous pimple to disappear before your Friday night study date, pray about it. If you're trying to decide where to go to college, pray for wisdom and guidance. If you're sitting home alone on a Saturday night, pray for a new friend to come into your life. Pray without ceasing as I Thessalonians 5:17 instructs.

Our lives are saturated with numerous prayer needs. It's so wonderful to have a God who hears and answers our every prayer. He's available 24/7. What more could you ask for?

Dear Lord,
I have only one wish.
Please, remove this blemish.
It grows lavishly on my face.
Oh, Lord, please grant me Your grace.
And rid me of this pimple,
That resembles a church steeple.
Amen.

What's the worst job you've ever had to endure? Maybe cleaning toilets as a maid, flipping burgers at McDonald's, or wiping babies' bottoms at a daycare. My worst job was working in the dish room at college. As the assembly line of dishes, cups, trays, and silverware paraded themselves in, my fellow survivors and I had to scrape and bang the dishes and trays free of the mushy and crusty leftover fragments. Then we were to stack them in the revolving racks in front and above our heads. The slow times were manageable. But at the end of lunch when classes were about to begin, the trays zoomed in without a lull. At times, our hands raced so quickly to swipe the plates free of food that scraps would fly onto our arms and faces. After my shift, I'd scurry to clean myself up in the fifteen minutes I had to get to my next class. But no matter how hard I tried, I still ended up sitting in class sweaty and smelling of rotten garbage.

What kept me going through this gross experience was the handbook we read during the hiring process. It instructed me that when I clocked into work, I was also clocking onto God's time clock. If I wasted time or allowed laziness to dominate my shift, it would also be a reflection of my work for the Lord.

The handbook closed with I Corinthians 10:31. "Whether therefore ye eat, or drink, or whatsoever ye do; do all to the glory of God." This verse encouraged me, showing me that all that I do is for God. And I couldn't let Him down.

So remember that *everything* you do is for God's glory—whether you're playing basketball, listening to your teacher in class, or cleaning your room. Do it for the Lord and not men. Even if it means washing another dish.

"If you're happy and you know it…" Can you finish this popular song? How about this one: "I'm a little teapot short and stout…"

Even though it's probably been eons since you've last heard these songs, I'm sure you didn't have any problem singing the rest of the words. Because songs are so catchy, they can stick with you for decades. This morning while driving to work, the radio announcer reported that by the time you're an adult, you will have memorized two thousand different songs. Can you even fathom how many different songs that is? If you started now, it would probably take you until *next week* to sing through every song.

Now just imagine how many Bible verses you'd be able to quote in a week's time. Will you know two thousand Bible verses when you're an adult? My friends and I have often commented how we wish Bible verses could be put to music. Then we would know so many more verses. But you can try it. Pick a verse, and pair it with a catchy tune. See how fast you can learn the verse.

Regardless of how you do it, learning and putting verses to use is essential for a Christian's growth. David learned verses to keep himself from sinning. (Psalm 119:11) Jesus told the Jews that knowing God's Word would show them the truth. (John 8:31-32) And, our faith grows by knowing God's Word. (Romans 10:17)

So keep memorizing verses. And whether you put them to music or write them with lipstick on your bathroom mirror, make sure that you are learning new verses every week. And before you know it, you'll be able to quote two thousand verses to the tune of "Happy Birthday."

Samson chose not to obey his parents' wishes for his future wife. They wanted him to marry a girl from among his people. But he desired a Philistine woman. Regardless of his parents' warning, his lust drove him to marry the Philistine. The result of his decision surrounded him with grief. At Samson's wedding feast, his new bride used her tears to con Samson into revealing his riddle. Then, she betrayed him to her people. After Samson angrily went on a killing spree, his bride was given to his friend to marry. A lot of heartache could have been avoided if Samson had just obeyed his parents' instruction. He may have even lived "happily ever after."

It's so important to obey your parents, even if they have a list of one hundred rules posted on the wall with rules like: 1. Bedtime is strictly at 10:30 P.M. 2. Curfew is mandatory for 10:00 P.M. 3. No boys allowed upstairs, EVER. Although your parents may seem too strict, they are only doing it for your benefit. I know this is hard to hear, but it's *true*. They have learned from their mistakes as teenagers and are only trying to help you avoid some of their pain. And when you become a parent, I'm sure you'll use all of the lessons you've learned to help guide *your* children. God also promises an extra bonus for obeying your parents. In Ephesians 6:3, God says that you will live longer just for heeding your parents' rules.

So although it may be difficult to obey your parents' rules, the blessings it will yield will make it well worth it.

And when you willingly obey your parents, it will make them happy. Maybe even happy enough to let you stay out until 11 P.M. next Friday night.

Every time the door opens, my heart flutters. Will the person behind the door listen or be upset that I interrupted his dinner hour? Will he be interested in what I'm saying or just want to slam the door in my face?

It's hard not to be fearful when you're witnessing to a stranger at his house. Even with your friends at school, it can be difficult to overcome worries that they will laugh at you or even stop being your friend because you witnessed to them. But witnessing is our duty as Christians. Although we may be scared, the *good news* is that God is with us, will strengthen us, help us, and uphold us. (Isaiah 41:10) He will give us the exact words to say to that unsaved friend. Or the encouragement to sing at church. Or the power to pray before school lunch, even with hundreds of scrutinizing eyeballs.

II Timothy 1:7 says, "For God hath not given us the spirit of fear; but of power, and of love, and of a sound mind." Fear comes from Satan. He will try to scare you out of being a witness and example of Christ. Don't let Satan rob you of the confidence God can and will give you if you ask. (Proverbs 3:26)

And as H. Jackson Browne so wisely put it: "Don't be afraid to go out on a limb. That's where the fruit is."[3] Just remember that there *are* rewards to witnessing and using your skills for Christ. And He *will* be with you every step of the way.

He provided a way across the Red Sea. Yet, they sinned. He led them through the wilderness with a cloud by day and fire by night. Yet, they sinned. He gave them water to drink from the rocks. Yet, they sinned. He supplied their desire for meat. Yet, they sinned. He rained sweet manna from Heaven. Yet, they sinned.

Through it all, God forgave the children of Israel. Not once or twice but *every* time they repented, God forgave them. What a blessed nation we are to have a God who forgives us 100% of the time. Even if we commit the same sin time after time, God will cleanse our hearts if we simply ask Him.

As humans, it would be nearly impossible for us to continue forgiving a friend who wronged us day after day. But that is what is so amazing about God. Everyday we sin against our Savior, but everyday He *still* forgives us. We never have to worry about God getting tired of taking us back into His arms.

Look at the children of Israel. God had blessed them and personally guided them through the wilderness, but they still fell into sin. God's extreme love allows Him to *want* to forgive us. After all, He loved us so much that He chose to die a horrible death on the cross to forgive us from *all* of our sins. Thank Him right now for what a truly loving and forgiving God He is.

Scriptures of the Day: Psalm 78, 86:5, 103:12, 1 John 1:9

Don't Choose the Krispy Kreme

It's a hypothetical situation, but what would you do if you won the lottery? It's thrilling to dream about what you would do with all of the loot. Would you purchase a mansion in Beverly Hills? Or a castle in England? Or even your own island in the Caribbean? But is there *anything* you would choose over the lottery money given the chance? Like a cancer cure, a warless world, or even the outlaw of abortion? It would be a tough decision to make, but what you love and care about the most would dominate your decision.

God's laws won David's heart. In Psalm 119:72, David said, "The law of thy mouth is better unto me than thousands of gold and silver." Given the choice, David would choose the Bible over millions of dollars. Could you say the same about yourself? Do you crave God's laws and His word as much as you crave that moist Krispy Kreme doughnut one week into your diet?

David even said in Psalm 119:131 that he panted for God's commandments. Just as much as a dog pants for that juicy steak, David panted for the law. David made the right decision. He would have rather had God's laws than all the money in the world. This says a lot about David's character. What does it say about yours?

Scripture of the Day: Psalm 119:72, 77, 92, 97, 127, 131, 162

Our church speaker recounted a story he had heard about a painting contest. The painters were competing to see who could best depict the idea of peace. When all of the canvasses had been turned in and judged, everyone was shocked to see that first place had been awarded to a painting of a raging storm. The remaining artists and spectators were so confused that they questioned the judge. He told them to look closely at the tree's branches.

Peering intently, the audience made out a bird's nest. A mother bird sat shielding her baby chicks from the storm with her wings. To the baby birds, all in the world was calm and at peace. Even though the winds were whipping sticks and leaves around them in the air, these babies were safe under their mother's wings.

Psalm 91:4 says, "He shall cover thee with his feathers, and under his wings shalt thou trust: his truth shall be thy shield and buckler." Just as the baby birds were protected with their mother's wings, we can be protected with God's wings. When the storms pound us from every way, we can find peace and safety under the strong wings of God. Flee to His side when your heart is broken and your strength is gone. He will keep you safe and dry in His haven of rest.

"Oh, God, please," I cried,
Begging Him to answer me.
"Please remove this thorn."
My sobs grew as I fell to my knees.

"My child, it is only for a time,"
His calm voice assured me.
"You know that I know all.
It is all part of My glorious plan for you."

I clutched my Bible closer to my aching heart.
A flattened rose petal fluttered to the floor.
Reaching through my tears, I scooped it up.
And then I heard Him quietly say,

"You see, My child, it is just like a rose.
There are trials, or thorns, that must be endured.
But in time, My time, a beautiful rose flourishes.
Sometimes, it just takes looking past the thorns to understand."

Scripture of the Day: II Corinthians 12:7-10

He Knows Your Favorite Shampoo

He knows your middle name. He knows when you have nightmares. He knows what you *really* want to be when you grow up. He knows when you are too shy to talk to your crush. He knows when your best friend makes you jealous. He knows about the little white lie you told your teacher.

God knows *everything* about you—from your shoe size to what shampoo you like. Knowing this can bring comfort or heartache depending on where you are in your Christian life.

As Christians, we can do a clever job of fooling the people around us into thinking that everything is perfect in our relationship with God. We can attend church, pray, read our Bibles daily, and participate in all of the other "required" Christian duties. Yet it's all pretend. Even though no one else around us knows the truth, God does. But don't let these thoughts scare you. Let them encourage you to strive to be closer to God.

Psalm 139:3 says, "Thou compassest my path and my lying down, and art acquainted with all my ways." Every step that you take, every dream that you dream, and every thought that you think, God is there—watching and loving you. In the times when you are alone or hurting, remember that God will *always* be with you. Let this strengthen your heart.

Scriptures of the Day: Psalm 44:21, Psalm 139, Matthew 10:29–31, II Timothy 2:19

How many different places have you lived in your life? Try to remember every apartment, trailer, house, etc. that you have lived in. So, how many? Maybe you have one place on your list. Maybe you have thirteen places. My list numbers ten different places in five different states. That's a lot of moving! But there is one more place that I know for sure I'll still have to add to my list—Heaven.

Do you know for sure that one day you'll live in Heaven? It's extremely important to make sure that you know. I thought I knew. When I was four, I asked Jesus into my heart in my Sunday school class. But that's what my parents told me. I never truly remembered doing it. Since then, I've heard numerous messages about the importance of being absolutely sure of your salvation. So when I was eleven, I knelt down on my bedroom floor and whole-heartedly confessed my sins and need for Jesus to be my Lord. And now I have such a sweet confidence and peace that my future home will be in Heaven.

Do you remember the time or place that you asked Jesus into your heart? If so, I'll see you in Heaven! But if you can't quite remember that experience, make sure of it today. It's so much better to be sure than to regret it later. So grab a friend, a parent, or just yourself, and ask Jesus to forgive you from all of your sins. Ask Him to prepare a place for you in Heaven with Him. If you pray, believing that Jesus can do all this—you will be saved *instantly*. And that is something to truly remember.

Scriptures of the Day: Romans 3:23, 6:23, 10:9-13, I John 5:13

Hope. A feeling we all experience constantly. Whether we're hoping for a good grade, for a call from that special someone, for snow, or just for our car to start—it happens frequently.

Recently, I was hoping to receive my "misplaced" suitcase back from the airport. (Yes, they had lost it!) I had just arrived back to college, and I was supposed to work the next day. But I had *no* bathroom supplies. I was a little stressed. Let me rephrase that. I bawled. In an attempt to calm down, I kept reminding myself that God knew where my suitcase was, and He would take care of me. And God did provide. I managed to make it through the next day with a few supplies from my purse and a few that were borrowed. Throughout the day, I kept hoping and praying that I would get my suitcase back. And guess what? It came! My prayers were answered.

Many times in life we lose hope in someone or something. But guess what? God will *never* disappoint you. He is Someone you can hope in for life, and He will *never* let you down. (Psalm 38:15) When trials grow thick, hope in God. You'll be happy you did. (Jeremiah 17:7)

Psalm 42:5 says, "Why art thou cast down, O my soul? and why art thou disquieted in me? hope thou in God: for I shall yet praise him for the help of his countenance." David found that hoping in God works. You can too.

Scriptures of the Day: Psalm 16:8-11, Psalm 39:7, Lamentations 3:24-25

Has your teacher ever had to tell you to pay attention? If so, I'm sure it embarrassed you enough to make you listen for the rest of class. Or at least the next ten minutes.

One thing I never really paid attention to was the words of hymns. I've sung them all my life—every Sunday, Wednesday, chapel, revival meeting, and missionary conference. I'm sure I've even sung them in my sleep a time or two. The problem with this is that the hymns can get so familiar that we're not even conscious of what we're singing about anymore.

This realization hit me one Sunday night after an altar call. After we had crooned "I Surrender All," my dad commented how he doesn't think people should sing this song because they probably haven't "surrendered all." Himself included. He thinks that the apostle Paul would probably have been one of the only ones that could've sung this song.

I mulled over his comments later, realizing that although I *have* given my life to God, I *haven't* surrendered my all. I don't always feel like telling my neighbors or coworkers the good news of Jesus. I don't always volunteer to help clean up after a church dinner. I don't always attend our church's nursing home services.

So now when the congregation turns to page 366, I usually join in the chorus with *I surrender Lord*. I'm trying to make this my prayer. *Every* day, I can try to surrender to His will.

Make it a habit to actively pay attention to the hymns you sing. Their words of comfort or praise will bless you. And then you can confidently belt it out, knowing every word you sing is true.

Several women at a party were chatting with the little daughter of their hostess. "I suppose that you are a great help to your mother," commented one of them.

"Oh, yes, ma'am," replied the child, "and so is Ethel; but today it's my turn to count the spoons after you have gone."[4]

Most young children adore helping their parents out with little jobs, whether "counting spoons" or sweeping the kitchen floor. They feel as if now they are a "big kid."

Just today, the little boy that I baby-sit enthusiastically remarked, "When I get big, I can wash the dishes so Daddy can watch TV. And I can do laundry, too!"

It's humorous how our excitement wanes as we grow older and realize that these "tasks" aren't as fun as they appear. But as we grow older, we do acquire more abilities that enable us to better help others.

Proverbs 3:27 says, "Withhold not good from them to whom it is due, when it is in the power of thine hand to do it." If you have the ability, time, or money to help someone, God says to do it. A couple of extra dollars in your pocket may help a friend finish paying for her school supplies. Your peacemaking skills could be very useful with your two arguing siblings. Some extra time could be used to take out the trash for your dad.

Helping others, without asking for anything in return, will bring joy to your heart as well as God's. And the more you help others, the more they may offer to help you out as well.

Life—the brevity of it—amazes me. And when a soul passes from its hold, the heartache can be unbearable. Sitting at the funeral home, I solemnly watch as hearts break and loved ones mourn for one now deceased. It was a tragedy. A suicide.

My eyes grow moist as bosom friends gather around the coffin one last time, holding and supporting each other with everything left in their souls. Though some try to hide the pain, others let it roll down their cheeks. Why did it have to be so sudden? So final? Death's hungry clutches are still waiting—desiring more. So now here we sit, alive yet sorrowful.

Night passes; morning comes. We huddle around the grave site to find warmth from not only the chill of the weather but also the chill of death. Last goodbyes are whispered to the soul now passed. Prayers escape to Heaven, asking for God's perfect peace.

One sad soul stands alone, gazing across the hills blanketed with corn stalks. Quietly, he contemplates death and life. A friend approaches, reaches his arms around him, and comforts his broken spirit.

A friend's hug helps to endure the grief. A friend's love makes it easier to get up the next morning. A friend's support will dry the flowing tears. And although one friend was lost today, the others who remain will grow more inseparable.

We find the power of love over death once more.

Love is strong as death.

Solomon

So what do you do? Scream? Pummel your pillow? Turn beet red? Use foul language? Take it out on your mom? Burst into tears? Throw a hissy fit? No matter how you choose to vent your anger, make sure that you are not sinning in the process.

Ephesians 4:26 says, "Be ye angry, and sin not…" Therefore, it is possible to be angry without sinning. The Bible shows us that when Jesus got angry at the moneychangers (Matthew 21:12-13) and when God got angry at the children of Israel for making a golden calf (Exodus 32:1-14), He did so *without* sinning.

We are very blessed to have a God who is slow to anger and ready to pardon us from our sins. (Nehemiah 9:17) With Jesus as our example, we can also be triumphant over our anger.

In Proverbs 15:1 it says, "A soft answer turneth away wrath: but grievous words stir up anger." By taking a moment to control your emotions, you can victoriously answer all those who anger you with a soft answer. Making a conscious effort to control your anger will please God. So, if you have to, throw that hissy fit *without* sinning.

"You Are Beautiful in My Sight"

Dear Jesus,

It's not fair. Why did I have to get stuck with frizzy red hair? I can never do anything with it! I wish I had hair like Heather's. All the guys love her long blond hair. And she doesn't have any pimples. Lord, please help my face to clear up before the school dance on Saturday. Then maybe Scott will ask me to be his date. He'll probably want to go with Heather though. She's so beautiful and so thin. It's not fair. Jesus, please help me to be pretty. Please!

Love, Rhonda

Dear Jesus,

I didn't make the basketball team today. Tryouts were rough! Coach Wilson told us to run three miles for warm-up. I couldn't keep up with the rest of the girls! I'm clearly not as in shape as the other girls at tryouts, especially Kara. All the guys gawk at her toned body. It's not fair, Jesus. I'm trying to stay in shape, but nothing seems to work. Please help me to feel better about myself.

Love, Angie

My Children,

I love you. I have created each of you in My perfect will. No feature is a mistake. I have made you just as I wanted you to be—unique. You are beautiful and special in My sight. Trust Me.

Love, Jesus

"A man sitting under a walnut tree was wondering why God had placed a large pumpkin on a small vine and a little walnut on a large tree. While he was philosophizing, a walnut fell from the tree and hit the man on the head. The man rubbed his head ruefully and said, 'I'm glad there aren't pumpkins up there.'"[5]

God knows what's best. Even when *we* don't agree. Romans 8:28a says, "And we know that all things work together for good to them that love God." There are many situations that arise in life when you simply want to ask, "Why are you doing this, God?" Like those times when your boyfriend dumps you or your algebra teacher just seems to have it out for you. Let me share a personal example.

This past summer, while trying to figure out how to pay for college, I was offered a chance to fly to New York City in order to write some articles for the upcoming memorial of September 11. I was to be paid $1,000, simply for working the last week of August. But this opportunity fell through. I wondered why God allowed this to happen. Didn't He want me to be able to help with college expenses? Later that day, my yearbook advisor called. She asked if I would be interested in being the writing editor for the yearbook (a *paid* position). My heart soared! I was going to get paid for a job I loved. Agreeing that I would, I was informed that I had to be back at school by the end of August. I then realized that if I had gone to New York City, I wouldn't have been able to accept the yearbook position because of the conflicting dates.

The Lord had provided. He knew what was best, and He showed me all this in *one* day. Sometimes when we go through disappointments or trials, we don't understand why. It may be that God has allowed a trial in our lives so that we might be able to later comfort those who are going through the same thing. (II Corinthians 1:4)

So although you *do* know or *don't* know why you have experienced a specific letdown in your life, trust God. He knows best. And He truly does make "all things work together for good."

They've been with you since birth. They've changed your diapers, burped you, kissed your "boo-boos," dried your tears, taken you to the zoo, thrown you slumber parties, driven you to and from basketball practice, pushed you to do your best in school, and *so* much more. But 99.9% of the time, we take them for granted. We think *oh, it's their job.* But it's not. Or... *I have plenty of time to say thank you.* But we may not.

Of course, parenting does come with responsibilities, but all of these things are done out of a pure love for their children. A parent's life is filled with daily tasks and responsibilities that are necessary to ensure a loving, well-provided home. And yet, they receive so little in return.

Sometimes a simple "thank you" would be sufficient to them. Or an "I love you." Or taking the trash out the *first* time you were asked. Or playing with your baby sister so your mom can take a much needed nap.

Show your parents that you appreciate all that they have done for you. Obedience goes a long way to show that you respect them. (Colossians 3:20) It's easier than you think, and in the process, you'll make them proud to call you their own. Let them have the privilege of bragging about you to their friends.

And thank them as often as you can. You never know, one morning you might wake up and find that one of them is gone. This horrifying experience happened to my college roommate last summer. One morning, a policeman knocked on her family's front door, breaking the news that their dad had just died in a car wreck.

She never got to say "goodbye" or "thank you" one last time. My heart breaks at the thought of this ever happening to one of my parents. I couldn't imagine life without them. They've done so much for me. The least I can do is to tell them so.

We had to wait 552 days for ours. Some only have to wait 365 days. And some only 180 days. But *every* bride-to-be counts the days until her wedding day.

Life is composed of waiting. Waiting in the doctor's office an hour after your appointment time. Waiting for your mom to finish her errands so that you can go to your friend's house. Waiting for your food to arrive at your favorite restaurant. Waiting can be extremely difficult especially if it affects a significant situation in your life. When my fiancé and I were engaged those 552 days, many of them were spent anxiously waiting on God to provide a job for my husband-to-be. We didn't even know where to look for a place to live because we didn't know if we'd have to move or not for his future job. It is *very* hard to keep praying and waiting and waiting and waiting day after day.

But Isaiah 40:31 (my favorite verse) says, "But they that wait upon the Lord shall renew their strength; they shall mount up with wings as eagles; they shall run, and not be weary; and they shall walk, and not faint." What a comfort this verse can be to us if we heed its instruction. God will give us the strength to keep waiting day after day. It's also comforting to know that everything is in God's perfect plan. When it's supposed to happen, it'll happen. This knowledge did comfort me in the crazy time of planning our wedding.

Another cool promise in Lamentations 3:25 says that

the Lord is good to those who wait on Him. So even though you may be sweating through one situation, the Lord will be blessing you in numerous others. So don't panic, relax and wait on Him. Even if it takes another 552 days.

My brain swam with thoughts. If I didn't know better, I would seriously think that each of my thoughts were sharks, attacking each other to be the most domineering.

Tossing once more on my bed, I turned to look at the clock. The red numbers 12:45 a.m. glared tauntingly at me. I sighed in frustration. Although I was exhausted, my numerous concerns and worries wouldn't let me fall asleep.

We've all had these moments in our lives. Some more than others. And, boy, are they annoying! Nights when you're extremely tired, yet you *still* can't quite make it to dream land.

But there *is* a solution. It's found in Psalm 94:19, a verse I've become quite familiar with. It says, "In the multitude of my thoughts within me thy comforts delight my soul." When I first came across this verse, I knew God had to have been pointing it out to me. It was perfect! Amid all our thoughts and worries, God is always there, ready to comfort us. All we have to do is ask.

One wearisome day, my then fiancé Brian and I decided to write all of our worries on a piece of paper. We read Psalm 94:19 before asking God for His comfort. Then we prayed for each other's lists. Committing them over to God, we ripped up our lists. A weight lifted off my shoulders, and I felt peace that everything was going to be okay. All of my troubles were now in God's hands. Not mine.

Scriptures of the Day: John 14:27, Philippians 4:7

The next time your thoughts are swimming, try making a list and giving it to God. He'll comfort you like you never thought possible with a peace that passes all understanding.

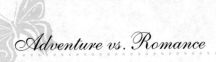
The beginning of a book will either capture or diminish your interest from wanting to read the rest of the book. Authors will agonize over each word, comma, and sentence before they feel peace about their book lead. Lately, I've been trying to find new authors to read. But many of the books I've randomly chosen, I decided to stop reading after the first couple of pages. It's the author's job to reach and keep his audience's attention.

One book that you should always be excited to read is God's book. He has given us so many interesting stories to read. Not only are His stories entertaining, but we can also learn from them. Stories like what happens to a man when he gets thrown into a den of lions. (Daniel 6) Or how a beautiful woman saves her people from getting slaughtered. (Esther) Or how a woman gets turned into a pillar of salt. (Genesis 19:1-29)

Every word in the Bible is placed there for a reason. (II Timothy 3:16) And through the stories, we can learn valuable life lessons. So whether you want a thrilling adventure or a romantic love story, the Bible has it all. Go read a story right now.

Scripture of the Day: I Kings 18:17-39

Back in 1835, fabulous Delmonico's Restaurant in downtown New York served the following menu:[6]

Cup tea or coffee	1 cent
Bowl tea or coffee	2 cents
Soup	2 cents
Fried or stewed liver	3 cents
Hash	3 cents
Pies	4 cents
Half pies	2 cents
Beef or mutton stew	4 cents
Beef steak	4 cents
Liver and bacon	5 cents
Veal cutlet	5 cents
Chicken stew	5 cents
Ham and eggs	10 cents
Hamburger steak	10 cents
Roast chicken	10 cents
Regular dinner	12 cents

Can you imagine feeding a family of five on a measly sixty cents? How incredible would it be to have the prices from the 1800s be our current prices! Then we would all be driving Mercedes and shopping at Tiffany's. Although it's impossible for prices to stop changing, we *can* count on Someone who will *never* change. Malachi 3:6a says, "For I am the Lord, I change not."

Scriptures of the Day: Psalm 102:26-27, Hebrews 1:10-12, Hebrews 13:8

How comforting it is to have a Savior who will never change or break His promises to us. We will *never* have to worry about God not forgiving our sins. (I John 1:9) Or not listening to us. (Psalm 34:4) Or not being with us. (Isaiah 41:10) Or not loving us. (John 3:16) And the list goes on! So even if your parents are in the midst of a divorce, or you have to switch schools, or your best friend just found a new best friend, take comfort in the truth that God will *never* change. That's His promise, not mine.

Little Johnny was in one of his very bad and disobedient moods. In answer to his mother's remonstration that he behave himself, he said: "Give me a quarter, and I'll be good."

"Give you a quarter!" she scolded. "Why Johnny, you shouldn't be good for a quarter, you should be good for nothing—like your father."[7]

This humorous story portrays a mother's poor attempt to encourage her son to follow his father's example. Being a good example *does* take a lot of hard work, especially for the Christian. Whether you realize it or not, your unsaved friends, family members, and classmates are watching you. It is extremely important that you find the right example to follow, so that others may also follow you.

Even if your dad or mom's Christian example has disappointed you at times, you do have a Father's example that is perfect to emulate. With Jesus as your shining example, you can better show the world how a Christian should act.

One list of Christ's attributes that I've tried to mirror is in Romans 12:9-21. One of our guest speakers at college suggested dividing these verses up and writing one trait each on a sticky note or note card. Then he told us to stick them on the bathroom mirror or anywhere else that we would see them frequently during the day.

Try to incorporate this exercise into your life. Then practice applying one trait a week. By the end of the

Scriptures of the Day: Philippians 2:2-5, I Timothy 4:12, I Peter 2:21-25

week, you'll be surprised how much more aware you are of that chosen trait. By using Christ's attributes in Romans (or anywhere else in the Bible), we can better reflect Christ's example of how a Christian should live.

"Don't worry. Be happy." This popular slogan can be found on badges, t-shirts, hats, and even license plates. It's a slogan that often gets spoken without a second thought about what it *really* means. But those four little words hold *so* much truth.

God tells Christians not to worry. Philippians 4:6 says, "Be careful for nothing; but in every thing by prayer and supplication with thanksgiving let your requests be made known unto God." Instead of worrying, we should give our fears and doubts to God. God will then give us a wonderful, unexplainable peace (vs. 7). Don't worry that God won't take care of your problems. He will. And He'll do what's best for you.

It's like the story of Helen Hayes, an actress, who made her first turkey on Thanksgiving for her family. "Before serving it she announced to her husband, Charles MacArthur, and their son James: 'Now I know this is the first turkey I've ever cooked. If it isn't any good, I don't want anybody to say a word. We'll just get up from the table, without comment, and go out to a restaurant to eat.' Then she returned to the kitchen. When she entered the dining room bearing the turkey, she found her husband and son seated at the table with their hats and coats on. Obviously they didn't have much faith in her ability to cook a turkey!"[8]

Sometimes we are just like Helen's husband and son. We'll give God our worries, but we won't fully trust

Him. He *knows* what He's doing with our lives. Give God *all* your worries so that you can truly be happy!

Casting All Your Care upon God, for He Careth for You[9]
By Thomas Washbourne

Come, heavy souls, oppressed that are
With doubts, and fears, and carking care.
Lay all your burdens down, and see
There's one that carried once a tree
Upon his back, and, which is more,
A heavier weight, your sins, he bore.
Think then how easily he can
Your sorrows bear that's God and man;
Think too how willingly he's to take
Your care on him, who for your sake
Sweat bloody drops, prayed, fasted, cried,
Was bound, scourged, mocked, and crucified.

Did you know that if you saved just ten dollars a week for ten years, you'd have saved $5,200. That's enough to buy a car. Or travel to Italy. Or plan a wedding.

Are you saving your money right now for college tuition, a new car, or even that pink prom gown? When God blesses you with extra cash, do you blow it so fast that Lincoln and Washington get whiplash? Or do you save it wisely?

Saving and being a good steward of our money *is* necessary and important. As Christians, we are commanded to tithe ten percent of any income received to the Lord. Even though it may seem like too much to give at the time, we should do it anyway—cheerfully.

I've heard numerous times in church messages that God can do more with your ninety percent than you can do with your one hundred percent. God will bless you for being obedient to Him. Don't be a frivolous spender, be a good steward of God's money. After all, it belongs to Him anyway. He's just letting us borrow it.

Movies like *Cinderella* along with TV shows like *Tom and Jerry* have depicted mice to be cute, cuddly, and friendly. Who could forget adorable little Gus (along with his friends) who worked so diligently to construct a beautiful dress for Cinderella?

But I'm sure if *you* ever happened to see a mouse scurry across your bedroom floor, you'd be on top of your bed in a second flat, screaming for your daddy. Mice definitely lose their appeal when they scamper around *your* house. To cure this problem, Americans have purchased mouse traps, mouse repellants, or even a cat. One website recommended spreading bubble gum around the house because mice can't digest it, and it would eventually lead to their death.

People will take many steps to rid the mice from their lives. So also should Christians take many steps to rid the sin from their lives. Sin is ugly and not welcomed in God's eyes. We should be as diligent in purging the sin from our lives as we are with purging the mice from our homes.

So flee from the sin that entices you. (II Timothy 2:22) Commit yourself to God, and resist the Devil. (James 4:7) Ask a friend to become your accountability partner. Most importantly, confess your sin to God and ask for His forgiveness. (I John 1:9) Do everything that you can to clean out the sin from your heart. The result? A spotless home in which God may dwell. Free of mice! Free of sin!

Almighty
Begotten
Caring
Deliverer
Eternal
Faithful
Glorious
Holy
Infinite
Judge
King
Loving
Merciful
Nurturing
Omniscient
Powerful
Quick
Redeemer
Sovereign
Trustworthy
Understanding
Victorious
Wise
Xtra gracious
Yearning
Zealous

Scriptures of the Day: Psalm 8, 100, 115

There are *so* many additional words that could have been used to describe God. I'm sure several of these characteristics reverberate close to your heart. God means countless things to each one of us. Try to comprehend today what a truly awesome God you serve.

Did you know that in Illinois a young person can get *arrested* for not heeding their parent's curfew? Did you know that 30% of American's favorite flavor of ice cream is vanilla? Did you know that there are around 8,400 different species of birds in the world?

Although minute, facts can be fun or boring. I've always loved learning new "Did you know?" facts from television, magazines, and books. They interest me. But did you know that the Bible is *filled* with thought-provoking facts? Many times because I've read a verse repeatedly, I'll just skim over it instead of *really* paying attention to every word. And by doing this, I'll miss something that's truly interesting.

Have you ever considered what Heaven would look like with windows? (Genesis 7:11)

Or... what God would have looked like riding on a cherub? (Psalm 18:10)

Or... what it must have been like to wander in the wilderness during the winter with only tents for shelter?

Or... what a turtle's voice sounds like? (Song of Solomon 2:12)

Or... what in the world a "pate" is? (Psalm 7:16)

There are numerous details in the Bible that can get skipped if you're not paying close attention. That's why it's so important to take the time to carefully read, meditate, and learn from *each* verse you read. Otherwise, you'll never stop to think what kind of clothing grass wears. (Matthew 6:30)

Try to find a thought-provoking fact. Share it with a friend. Discuss your ideas. Most importantly, soak in as much as you can of God's Word. And remember, *every* word has been written for a purpose.

9/15
Dear Jesus,

I had a bad day today. I'm so tired of people, Lord. Why do they always have to let me down? Jenny's going out with Tom now. She always told me that things wouldn't change between us when she got a boyfriend. Well, she lied. She never wants to hang out with me anymore, and when I do see her all she talks about is Tom this and Tom that. Now what am I going to do on Friday nights? Help me, Lord, to not be so lonely.

Love, Anna

9/17
Dear Jesus,

At church tonight, Pastor preached about how You are always there for us and how You are our best friend. I realized then that You have always been my best friend, and You will always be my best friend. I'm so glad I don't have to worry about You deserting me. Thank you for being my comfort. Please help me to find my sufficiency in You, not through my friends.

Love, Anna

9/18
Dear Jesus,

Today I introduced myself to the new girl in our class. She looked lonely. Her name is Tina. I asked her if she wanted to go to the mall with me on Friday night. She said yes! And guess what. She lives just down the road from me! Thank you, Lord, for my new friend. And thank you for being my best friend.

Love, Anna

9/19

Dear Jesus,

Jenny asked to hang out with me and Tina tonight because Tom wanted to hang out with his friends. I told her she could.

Love, Anna

He loves you. Or so he promised. She said she would always be there for you. But now she hangs out with Lisa and never talks to you. Your brother promised to pick you up at four o'clock from the mall, but he forgot.

People continually make promises, but many times, they break them. There is Someone who will *never* break His promises. Judges 2:1b says, "I will never break my covenant with you." Deuteronomy 7:9 says, "Know therefore that the Lord thy God, he is God, the faithful God, which keepeth covenant and mercy with them that love him and keep his commandments to a thousand generations."

Many times in Scripture, we see examples of God keeping His promises. In Genesis 9:9-17, God made a promise to Noah that He would never flood the earth again. To show that He would keep His promise, God said He would put a rainbow in the sky every time it rained. In Genesis 15, God promised to make Abraham's descendants as numerous as the stars in the heavens. In I John 2:25 and Titus 1:2, God promised to give us eternal life. In Hebrews 13:5b, God promised that He would never leave us or forsake us.

We *never* have to worry about God breaking his promises. He doesn't lie. (Hebrews 6:18) So anytime you come across a promise from God in the Bible, have faith that God will keep it. He will never let you down.

The sun had just finished sinking into the horizon, leaving behind an array of pinks, oranges, and yellows. The warm air surrounded David as he stepped out onto his flat rooftop. It had been a trying day, and David simply wanted to relax. Wandering in circles, he fell deep into thought. *Should I have gone into battle? Is my kingdom disappointed in me?*

David came to the edge of the roof. He glanced around, not really knowing what he was looking for. Out of the corner of his sparkling eyes, his glance fell on a beautiful woman washing herself. He turned quickly, hot embarrassment flooding his well-toned body. *I need to leave now. I shouldn't be here. But one more glance wouldn't hurt.* David turned again, watching every move of the woman. Watching as she rinsed the soap from her soft pale skin. *I must learn who she is. I must be with her.*

David fell into sin that day. He never planned on it. No one would have expected it from such a godly king. But he happened to be in the wrong place at the wrong time. (II Samuel 11:1) No one ever plans to fall into sin's clutches. That's why we must prepare ourselves beforehand never to let ourselves get into those "tempting situations."

II Timothy 2:22 says, "Flee also youthful lusts: but follow righteousness, faith, charity, peace, with them that call on the Lord out of a pure heart." I Peter 2:11 says we should abstain from fleshly lusts. It's hard to say no when you're staring temptation in the face. That's why the Bible says to *flee* lusts. According to the American Heritage College Dictionary (third edition), flee means "to run away, as from trouble or danger."

Temptation is dangerous, but we can overcome it with God's help. God doesn't allow us to be tempted anymore than we can handle. *And* He provides a way of escape. (I Corinthians 10:13) By leaning on Christ and asking Him for strength, we *can* overcome temptation. And Jesus promises a crown of life to all those who endure testing. (James 1:12) Look to Jesus for power to conquer temptation. He will provide it—if you ask.

It's composed of 86,400 seconds. Sometimes these seconds fly by, but many times, they drag by. It just depends on what you're doing.

Most of the time, we are wishing away these seconds—seconds that make up our day. Especially at this time of life, we want time to fly by until graduation, until college is over, or until we get married. Even for the smaller things in life, like parties, birthdays, weekends, and Christmas breaks, we yearn for time to fly by. It's wonderful to look forward to things in life, but we shouldn't wish time away.

Psalm 118:24 says, "This is the day which the Lord hath made; we will rejoice and be glad in it." God has created each day for us to enjoy. Even on our worst days when everything is going completely wrong, there is a reason and purpose for that day. God has made every day equal.

My youth director once commented that every day is a gift from God. That's why it's called "the present." That thought has always stuck with me. Every time I start wishing time away, I try to remember that God has created each day for our enjoyment. The cool thing is that you never know when something truly amazing could happen. Like getting that guy to finally talk to you. Or your parents complimenting you on what a good daughter you are. Sometimes it *is* those "boring" days when something good happens. So every time you wake up, try to remember that God has created *this* day for a purpose.

Dear Pastor,

I just wanted to let you know how much I appreciate all that you do for our church. I know that often you get so busy with church-related things that you don't get to relax and have much down time. But everything you do—from visiting the shut-ins on your day off to helping clean up the church after anniversary and graduation parties—is noticed and appreciated.

Your true love for God and your people is evident on your face every time you speak at the pulpit. It thrills my soul to see such a man of God openly and wholly sharing his heart. I've grown so much since I first started attending this church with my parents. Every message from God you bring fits my exact need for that time of my life.

I'm praying for you to have the wisdom to make the important decisions, time to accomplish what each day holds, a stronger love for your people, and a desire to continue growing. Thank you so much for everything you do for our church ministry. I know God has a special crown for you in Heaven.

Love and Prayers,
An appreciative soul

Pastors are those with an endless job. They don't even have the chance to "leave everything at the office." Write your pastor (or even your youth pastor) an encouraging letter—just to let him know that he is loved and appreciated. It will make his day.

Scripture of the Day: Jeremiah 3:15

Baked in Sweat

The last five minutes in a tanning bed for me are usually torturous. Especially my first visit back after a long winter season. The sweat slides off of my body like hot butter off corn on the cob. The heat from the tanning bed bulbs bake me to an even 350 degrees on both sides—just like my favorite casserole. And although I'm counting the seconds until relief will come, it is all for a reason. I make myself uncomfortable in order to reward myself with a nice tan—usually just before a wedding I'm participating in or our upcoming summer vacation.

But just like I have a choice to stop being uncomfortable if I wished to, so also do we as Christians have a choice to walk away from an uncomfortable situation. It's our choice. We can choose to be surrounded by things we know are wrong, or we can get up and get away from the sins that are enticing us.

After we are saved, the Holy Spirit dwells inside each one of us. He allows feelings of conviction to consume our minds in order to get us to flee from the sinful lures. And although we may be uncomfortable feeling this way, it is a blessing. For when we feel this way, we know that the Holy Spirit is working on us—molding us into stronger Christians. So be thankful for those times of uneasiness. And make sure that you get out of those situations before it's too late.

Scriptures of the Day: Genesis 39:1–12, Ephesians 1:13–14

Another day of fishing. That's what the agenda held for Simon and his brother Andrew. Casting their nets into the water and then the waiting. Always the waiting. As Simon and Andrew flung their nets out one last time, they heard a powerful voice call to them.

Looking up, they stared straight into the eyes of Jesus. "Come ye after me, and I will make you to become fishers of men." (Mark 1:17)

And do you know what they did? Without hesitating, they chose to follow Christ. Mark 1:18 says "And straightway they forsook their nets, and followed him." Their decision was immediate. They didn't stop to think if they had the time or skills to follow Christ. They just did it. Even their occupation didn't hold them back. They left their nets in the sea without a thought or care.

So what would you have done in this situation? Continued to fish? Would you have had "nets" holding you back? Whatever your nets may be, get rid of them. Our purpose in life is to follow Christ anytime and anywhere. He is the reason we live and breathe. So don't get caught under a net, be ready. Always.

Scriptures of the Day: Matthew 9:9, Mark 1:16-20

Are you jealous of Sharon's perfect nose? Or Jill's Abercrombie jeans? Or Christy's toned tummy? Or even Kari's Gucci handbag?

It is extremely difficult not to compare our bodies and status with other girls, especially with Hollywood pushing the market of plastic surgery.

Episodes of the *Fabulous Life of...* (a series on VH1) show us that when Puff Daddy bought a 35 million dollar house, he threw a $430,000 party to celebrate. And when Britney Spears gets her haircut, she uses $3,000 imported scissors!

It made me sick to see the money that these stars have and how flippantly they spend it. I finally had to stop watching these programs for a while. Jealousy had crept into my heart, causing me to covet worldly possessions and physical beauty. Although I was very happy and content at that time in my life (I had just gotten married to the man of my dreams!), I started coveting what these "stars" had. I wanted more.

As Christians, we are commanded not to covet. (Exodus 20:17) By not heeding this command, we are sinning. Coveting or being jealous of Jill's Abercrombie jeans is not from God. (I John 2:16) Do not let Satan win the battle of your heart. Fight against him, whether it be changing the channel or exercising a little more to get that "tight tummy." And remember, true contentment comes only from God.

It's been a long week. One hundred and sixty-eight hours to be exact. It's one of those things that you don't really appreciate until it's gone, as the saying goes. My car had to be towed to the repair shop last Monday because it wouldn't start. Of course it decided to start when the mechanic tried to find the problem. I seriously think my car has a mind of its own. It's been messing with my head for about a month now. Even the needles on my odometers act crazy. Out of nowhere, they'll start moving back and forth, acting as if it's the most normal thing in the world. But I don't think it's very comical.

Just like my car is broken and cannot be used, so also can we think that our Christian lives are "broken" and cannot be used. We may think a past sin or failure puts a big black mark on our heart, and therefore, God can no longer use us. But the opposite is true. God still uses those with broken hearts and past failures. (Psalm 51:17b)

The Bible says in Psalm 147:3 that God heals broken hearts and bindeth up wounds. In Psalm 34:18, it says that God is nigh unto those with a broken heart. When you feel like you've committed the ultimate sin or anything that makes you feel not good enough to serve or be used by God, remember that God can heal your heart and make it whole again. He wants to use you.

Just like a potter carefully molds his piece to perfection so also does God mold our lives to His perfection. He is our Potter. He wants to make our lives valuable. Just ask Him to smooth out the bumps and bruises in your heart. Let Him mold your life into an exquisite masterpiece.

Dear Jesus,

I'm so lonely. Today at lunch I had to eat alone. When I do actually get to sit with some of the girls, they never talk to me. Even now at home I'm lonely. My mom's so busy with my new baby brother that she never has time for our girl talks anymore. And my dad's always at work. Sometimes I just curl up under my covers and bawl. I wish I had someone to talk to…

Your daughter,
Julie

Dear Julie,

I am that Someone. I am always with you. That is My promise. When you need someone to talk to, I am here listening, My child. So pour your heart out to Me anytime. You can depend on Me to be your Friend, Father, and Lord. I will dry your tears.

Love eternally,
Jesus

Scriptures of the Day: Joshua 1:5, Psalm 27:10, Proverbs 18:24b, Matthew 28:20b

Believing that God created the world in six days.

Trusting the pilot to safely fly you to Florida.

Knowing that your best friend would have your back in a fight.

Believing that Jesus will soon return.

Trusting that your McDonald's food doesn't have any unidentifiable objects in it.

Knowing that your wedding day will be perfect.

Believing that your mother's cancer will be healed.

Trusting that the rash on your legs will disappear before next week's pool party.

Knowing that everything happens for a reason.

Believing that you'll receive your paycheck every two weeks.

Trusting that you'll one day find the love of your life.

Knowing that the sun will come out tomorrow.

Believing that you'll get accepted at your first choice for college.

Trusting your parents to never get divorced.

Knowing that Jesus is the only true way to Heaven.

Faith is a knowledge within the heart,
beyond the reach of proof.
-Kahlil Gibran[10]

Scriptures of the Day: Matthew 17:19-20, Mark 10:52, Luke 17:5, Hebrews 11:1-3

A booming voice startles Jonah awake from his dream of catching a twenty pound fish. Rubbing his crusty eyes, he scans his 12'x12' room for the perpetrator that broke into his fantasy catch.

"Jonah." This time Jonah realizes it is God speaking to him.

"Yes, Lord?" he answers quizzically.

"I want you to go to the great city of Nineveh and preach repentance."

Jonah starts to shake. "Nineveh? How could I travel to such a wicked city and persuade them to repent?"

Everyone in Jonah's city knew of Nineveh's shameless ways. As stories were spread around town, Jonah and his friends would just shake their heads with grief. Needless to say, Jonah didn't catch anymore fantasy fish that night. He tossed and turned all night, haunted by nightmares of what Nineveh would hold. The next morning he sat up in a cold sweat—released from his night terrors yet strangled with fear.

That day Jonah decided to run from God. He chose not to obey God's command. But God always has a way to guide His wandering sheep back into the fold. God used a whale to redirect Jonah's thinking. And as soon as Jonah had the opportunity, he went straight to Nineveh carrying God's message. Like Jonah, we too will be chastened by God when we disobey His commands—until we get back on the right path. Just remember that He still loves you; He just has to do a little correcting.

Scriptures of the Day: Jonah 1:1–3, 3:1–3, Hebrews 12:5–7

I will never forget the "trials" of working at daycare. Is it normal for three and four-year olds to hit and cuss at you? Or spit in your ear? Or bite you? For me, it was just another day at work. I should have mass produced t-shirts reading "I survived working at daycare." I would have made enough to buy my dream wedding gown.

At that time, I couldn't look for another job because of surrounding circumstances. Like it or not, I was stuck. I felt God must be trying to teach me patience. I'd have to pray and beg God for patience and strength to get through certain days.

But Romans 5:3 says, "And not only so, but we glory in tribulations also: knowing that tribulation worketh patience." I don't know about "glorying in my tribulations" at the daycare, but it comforted me to know that my trials were molding me into a more patient person. Looking back now, I definitely have learned more patience when working with children! And the crazy thing is… I'm now working as a nanny.

So what trial are you going through right now? A nosey little sister reading your diary? Bad grades on your tests? Parents fighting every night? Hang tough, and lean on Christ. For as soon as the trial is through, you'll have learned patience. Even through all the bites and bruises.

Life is busy. That's definitely an understatement! As time passes, it seems that more and more needs to be done. Society has been trying to adapt to the fast-paced world. Inventions and services have been created to try to save people time—microwaves, fast food restaurants, the Internet, overnight delivery, and even maid services for all those who think they simply have "no time" to clean. But none of these things seem to help. America still rushes around frantically. The other day I read an advertisement for a book titled something like How to Cram 10 Hours into 8 Hours. I had to laugh. People write books about how to save time? I wonder where they found the time to write it!

During a busy day, it's easy to forget about spending quiet time with God. But amidst all the busyness, God should still be first on "our list". It doesn't take long to thank Him for a new day or to ask Him for strength to get through our day. Quiet time with God is a necessity. It prepares us for what lies ahead, and it helps us to get our focus straight.

I've often heard people comment that the days they did spend time with God—even when they didn't think they had the time—they accomplished much more than the days they didn't spend time with God.

Life is busy. So make spending time with God a priority.

Scriptures of the Day: Psalm 4:4, Psalm 46:10, Ecclesiastes 3:1-8

"I Didn't have Time"[11]

I got up early one morning
And rushed right into the day!
I had so much to accomplish
That I didn't take time to pray.

Problems just tumbled about me
And heavier came each task.
"Why doesn't God help me?" I wondered
He answered, "You didn't ask."

I woke up early this morning
And paused before entering the day,
I had so much to accomplish
That I had to take time to pray.

---Selected

For Pepperoni Pizza and Sweaters

It's mentioned 138 times in the Bible. (At least some form of the word.) I think God was trying to stress its importance. Anyone can do it, but most often, people forget. We should do it everyday—good days and bad days. We should definitely do it before eating a large pepperoni pizza. Or after receiving another sweater from Aunt Martha for Christmas.

I'm sure you've guessed by now that it's giving thanks. Ephesians 5:20 says, "Giving thanks always for all things unto God and the Father in the name of our Lord Jesus Christ;" We see here that we should not only give thanks when we receive something, but that we should be giving thanks always.

Do it when people are not expecting it. Try thanking your parents for always providing you with food, shelter, and clothing. You might just blow them away! Or thank your pastor or youth pastor for the wonderful job that they do preaching. Or thank your friends for always being there for you. People appreciate hearing "thank you." It's not hard to say, and it goes a long way.

God has blessed us with so much. Even on our bad days, we can thank God for food, water, shelter, clothing, life, and creation. And by doing this, sometimes a bad day can turn into a good day when we see how much we really do have to be thankful for.

Take time to thank God and others for what they have done for you. Maybe even make a list of one hundred things that you are thankful for and hang it up somewhere that you'll see often. This will help remind you to always be thankful for what you have been so graciously blessed with.

He sat on a bar stool, a beer in his hand. Having just been saved earlier that day, he didn't exactly know if drinking was wrong. Drinking happened to be a part of his life-style. But this particular night all that changed.

Suddenly, he felt a hand on his shoulder, as if pulling him from the bar stool. Putting the untouched beer down, he yielded to this unseen hand guiding him out of the bar. Since that day, he has never entered (or desired to enter) a bar again.

As my dad told me this story years ago, I sat mesmerized. He actually felt his guardian angel intervening in his life! I've always seen those little guardian angel pins in stores and heard that we all have angels protecting us, but it never fully hit me that every Christian has a guardian angel watching over them until I heard my dad's story.

Psalm 91:11-12 says, "For he shall give his angels charge over thee, to keep thee in all thy ways. They shall bear thee up in their hands, lest thou dash thy foot against a stone."

My English literature teacher also told me of the time his guardian angel protected him. He was standing on a curb, just about to cross the street. But he felt a hand on his shoulder pulling him back. Turning to see who it was, he saw no one. Just then, a car turned right, whizzing past him. If he hadn't felt the hand pulling him back, he would have stepped out right in front of the car. My teacher believes it was his guardian angel's hand saving his life.

God, out of the goodness of His heart, blessed us by giving us someone to continually watch over for us. Thank the Lord, today, for your guardian angel. You never know when you might feel a hand on your shoulder.

Okay, I know it's rather disgusting, but the other day on *The Oprah Winfrey Show* the conversation revolved around poop. Yes, poop! And no, she didn't run out of topics to talk about! My mother-in-law watched this episode and later reported what she had learned. Did you know that guys fart fourteen times a day? And get this. Did you know that girls also fart fourteen times a day? Yup, the same number of times as guys! I guess we're just a little more discreet about it.

Although it's not pleasant to talk or even think about, these bodily functions were created to clean wastes from our systems. Showers were created to clean our bodies from germs and dirt. And sometimes soap has been used to clean out mouths after dirty words have escaped. I'm not sure if you've ever had to experience this tactic for discipline. I guess I was lucky enough to only get the belt. Is that lucky?

Your tongue can get you into a lot of trouble—from cussing to gossiping to lying. James 3:8 says, "But the tongue can no man tame; it is an unruly evil, full of deadly poison." By now, your parents hope that you can control your tongue, but it's really up to you to carry it out. It's hard not to fluff a story about a friend when you have eight eager ears listening to you. It's hard not to let a little cuss word escape after you miss the bus the day of your class trip. It's hard not to lie when your parents ask you why you weren't home by curfew. But you do have power over your tongue to avoid these sins. With God's help, you can learn to tame it—before you have to spiritually get your mouth washed out with soap.

Scriptures of the Day: Job 6:24, Psalm 10:7, 34:13, James 3:5-10

Roses. Chocolate. Poetry. Perfume. All of these things are used to express love to one another, especially on Valentine's Day. Anytime you are given one of these gifts, you feel loved. (At least, I hope you do!) But all of these ways of communicating love are so insignificant compared to the way God chose to express His love for us. He sent His only son Jesus to die on the cross for us to save us from our sins (John 3:16). What love!

I can't imagine what it would be like to let my only child die a painful, horrible death. And I don't even have kids yet! But God did it anyway. He loved us that much. And He still does. It's comforting to know that no matter who hurts us, God is still there loving us.

Even when we sin and hurt God, He still wants to forgive us. All we have to do is ask. We can't do anything to make God stop loving us. His love is the ultimate love story. We don't need the roses or the chocolates to know that He loves us. It's written in His Word over and over again.

The Love of God [12]

Frederick M. Lehman
Arranged by Claudia L. Mays

The love of God is greater far
Than tongue or pen can ever tell;
It goes beyond the highest star,
And reaches to the lowest hell;
The guilty pair, bowed down with care,
God gave His Son to win;
His erring child He reconciled,
And pardoned from his sin.
Oh love of God, how rich and pure!
How measureless and strong!
It shall forevermore endure,
The saints' and angels' song.

Life is Short

My best friend called me this past weekend.

"Do you remember Katie?" she asked softly. "She used to go to high school with us."

"Yeah, I remember her. What about her?" I asked, wondering what was coming.

"She had a heart attack," Joni answered slowly. "She died unsaved."

My heart clenched. Not saved? But Katie had gone to our Christian school. She had heard numerous times how to be saved. I had assumed everyone at school was saved. But Katie wasn't.

This made me wonder—how many other "Katies" are out there? How many people do I come in contact with everyday who aren't saved? What about you? Do you know if the guy you sit beside in English class or the girl you work with at the mall is saved? Katie's life ended much earlier than she ever imagined. Perhaps she thought she had plenty of time to get saved, but from Scripture, we see that we aren't even promised tomorrow.

James 4:14 says, "Whereas ye know not what shall be on the morrow. For what is your life? It is even a vapour that appeareth for a little time, and then vanisheth away." Katie didn't have tomorrow. We may not either.

God commands Christians to tell others about Him and what He has done for them on the cross. So that someday, they, too, can live forever with Jesus. Life is short. No one knows when his time will be through. We must be diligent in spreading the good news of Jesus to everyone we meet. That way, another Katie won't slip by.

Scriptures of the Day: Ecclesiastes 2:1-11, 12:13-14

I was fifteen. He was in his fifties. I thought I had it rough having to walk ten miles in the blazing sun. But he had to run twenty-six! During these ten miles, I longed for a drink of water. I can't imagine how desirous he must have been for even one sip of water.

Just like my youth director and I thirsted for water, so also did David thirst after God. Psalm 63:1 says, "O God, thou art my God; early will I seek thee: my soul thirsteth for thee, my flesh longeth for thee in a dry and thirsty land, where no water is."

We should thirst for God as much as we would thirst for a glass of ice-cold water after a twenty-six mile run. After all, God should be our first love. Like the bride who longs for her wedding day, the teenage guy for his first car, and a woman for her first baby, so also should we long for God.

There are many ways to draw closer to God. We can find a special, quiet place to meet and commune with God every day. We can write God love letters, expressing our appreciation for all He is and does. We can sing praise choruses and hymns, meditating on each word we sing.

God should be our greatest desire in life. He has given us so much. As you go throughout the day, may your heart and mind reflect the words of one of my favorite choruses: "As the deer panteth for the water so my soul longeth after Thee. You alone are my heart's desire, and I long to worship Thee."[13] I'm thirsty. How about you?

The white sandy beaches. The sparkling blue ocean water. The bliss of sleeping in. No cooking, cleaning, or laundry. Total relaxation. Can you tell that I'm a little overjoyed about our upcoming Florida vacation? Just the thought of the tranquility and relaxation that it will yield thrills my heart. Even though 129 days separate me from my vacation, I daydream about it often—when the dishes resemble the game of Jenga in my sink, when the kids I baby sit are fighting over a bathtub toy, when life never seems to allow a breather.

But did you know that there's something much more important that we all should be looking forward to? No, it's not that awesome sales job, brand new silver Mustang, or glamorous outdoor wedding. (Although these things are wonderful.) It's the return of our Lord Jesus Christ. Are you "counting the days" until He comes back?

Like myself, I'm sure you want to experience some of the great joys in life before He returns. It's natural and human to feel this way. God understands. But these things shouldn't totally block your anticipation of Christ's return. When He comes again, we will no longer have to worry about feeling any pain or sickness. We'll be living a perfect life in Heaven. And that's something to get excited about. It will be a trillion times better than any Caribbean vacation we can dream up. Heaven is Paradise! So look forward to His return with more zeal than you would your ultimate dream vacation.

What was Jesus thinking,
When Judas turned an act of love into betrayal?

What was Jesus thinking,
When the mobs chose to free Barabbas instead of Him?

What was Jesus thinking,
When He was stripped of His purple robe?

What was Jesus thinking,
When He was hanging on the cross between two thieves?

What was Jesus thinking,
When He was lying in the sepulcher?

But when Jesus arose victorious,
What was the world thinking?

We will never know the thoughts and reactions from all those who took part in Christ's crucifixion. We will never know the realization and horror the people felt when they were told of Christ's victory from the grave. But now, we do know the greatest story ever told. Do not hesitate to tell others that Jesus did not remain in the grave, but that He arose triumphantly over sin and death. Rejoice, O Christian, rejoice!

Scriptures of the Day: Matthew 20:17-19, Luke 24:1-12, 44-48

My Prayer

Dear Jesus,

Thank you for being my Strength. I know I couldn't have made it through today without You. The day seemed to stretch on forever, not offering any enjoyment or rest. I felt like bedtime was never going to come. But through it all, I felt Your calming peace around me. As I prayed for strength and comfort, I knew You were listening, waiting to answer my prayer. And when I felt lonely, I knew You were beside me, holding my hand. Thank you, Jesus.

On these days, I feel so close to You. Is it because I need You more? Lord, I pray that even on my carefree, happy days, I will feel as close to You as I do now.

Jesus, You're amazing. How do You listen to everyone's prayers at once? How does Your love spread to everyone so that we all feel exclusively loved? Although I'll never understand it, I'm so glad it's possible. I love You, Lord. Help me to encourage others with Your strength so that they, too, can feel Your presence and comfort. Bless tomorrow's challenges. Help me to lean only on You.

Love, Me

Scriptures of the Day: Psalm 18:32, Isaiah 49:13, II Corinthians 12:9

Even the Birds Know

Gazing out my airplane window, I watched as the glowing fireball slowly sank in the sky. Colorful arrays of pink, purple, and blue stretched across the sky's tapestry. As we soared steadily above the clouds, I couldn't help but be awed by God's handiwork. It was like a hush had come over my soul—a hush of wonder and worship. And to think that many people don't even believe that there is a God! Couldn't they see, even through a sunset, that Someone much bigger than them had to orchestrate it?

My thoughts were interrupted by a man on my left. As if in awe also, he murmured, "Maybe this is why birds sing all the time, because they get to see sights like this everyday." His statement held so much truth. Even the birds knew of God's glory.

Creation boldly proclaims and uplifts God's name to the entire world. Everywhere we look—from the sparkling starlit nights to the white snowcapped mountains—nature's beauty shouts God's name. And He's made everything for us to take pleasure in. Take time to really enjoy nature and its every aspect. Let it show you that there truly is a God. A God who loves you. A God worthy to be praised.

Scriptures of the Day: Psalm 19:1, Psalm 148

All Things Bright and Beautiful[14]
Cecil Frances Alexander

All things bright and beautiful,
All creatures great and small,
All things wise and wonderful,
The Lord God made them all.

Each little flower that opens,
Each little bird that sings,
He made their glowing colours,
He made their tiny wings.

The purple-headed mountain,
The river running by,
The sunset, and the morning
That brightens up the sky,

He gave us eyes to see them,
And lips that we might tell
How great is God almighty,
Who has made all things well.

One of a writer's trademarks is that they're always carrying a notepad. In their moments of inspiration at the train station, video store, or even in the bathroom stall, it's crucial that they can quickly write down their thoughts. Otherwise, waiting until their next destination could prove to be too late. Thus defusing their next would-be best seller.

But in those times of desperation, writers may innovatively use a napkin, receipt, or parking pass to jot down a few notes. Then later, they could write it out in detail. Taking notes and writing down ideas is a necessary part of a writer's life. It's second nature to them. It should be second nature to us also.

Hebrews 2:1 says, "Therefore we ought to give the more earnest heed to the things which we have heard, lest at any time we should let them slip." We need to be diligent in writing down the truths we find in God's Word. We need to have our pencils ready to jot down the gems we hear in our pastor's Sunday night message. Anytime and anywhere we should be ready to write down a truth or insight that God gives us. By writing these thoughts down, we can not only share them with others but we can also review them ourselves when we need them the most.

It's also important to write down the prayer requests and praises that you have. Then in a few months, when you need a little encouragement, you can remember the glorious blessings you received. It will be so rewarding to read the pages over and over again.

God is good. These three words are mentioned many times, but do we ever really realize the simple truth that they hold? Everyday, God gives us more blessings than we deserve. Even during a bad day, His love and blessings are evident. Yet many times we don't think to thank Him for all He has done for us.

It doesn't take long to say a prayer of thanksgiving—probably just a few minutes. But even if you feel like you don't even have an extra few minutes during the day, you can praise God on your way to school, in the shower, or while you're waiting in line at the store.

The Lord has given us so much. Take a minute right now to praise Him for life today. For green grass. For daffodils. For laughter. For best friends. For chocolate. For bubble baths. For family. For books. For hugs. For long walks. For hour-long phone conversations.

There are so many things we can praise the Lord for everyday. Even if we haven't killed a giant or won any battles, we can still join King David in proclaiming, "I will praise thee, O Lord, with my whole heart; I will show forth all thy marvellous works. I will be glad and rejoice in thee: I will sing praise to thy name, O thou most High." (Psalm 9:1-2) Praise the Lord today!

The Subway Diet. The Raw Foods Diet. The Peanut Butter Diet. The No Carb Diet. The Dash Diet. The Atkins Diet. These diets represent only six of the sixty-four listed plans on a dieting website. And this was the only website I browsed. At least Americans have a variety to pick from!

Americans are faced with the ever growing demand for low fat, non fat, zero carb, and low cal foods. We definitely need all the help we can get. Last Sunday, my husband and I saw an ambulance at Golden Corral, a popular buffet restaurant. The paramedics were wheeling a customer on a stretcher out from the restaurant. My husband jokingly remarked that the person had probably eaten too much. True or not, it was sad to witness.

As Christians, physical exercise is not the only type of exercise we should be concerned about. We should also be exercising spiritually. Our bodies are God's temples. (I Corinthians 6:19-20) Because He's dwelling within us, we have to be cautious not to use or do anything that will bring harm to our bodies. Don't let sin set up house in your heart. Sweep it out with prayers of confession. Equip yourself with Bible verses so that you can fight off the lures of Satan. Keep your energy level high by taking quiet time to meditate on all of God's blessings.

Although it's important to stay in good physical condition, it's even more important to stay in good spiritual condition. So use your time wisely. Take a mile walk

Scriptures of the Day: I Timothy 4:8, III John 2

through the park, but do so with a prayer of thanksgiving on your lips. While bike riding with a friend, take turns quoting Bible verses to each other. Do one hundred sit-ups while listening to your favorite praise CD. Get tough—physically and spiritually!

I had called 1-800-555-TELL to find out the current temperature in Uniontown, Ohio. The recorded voice informed me that it was 50 degrees. Although it was cool enough to wear a jacket, I was about to let Sam and Katie (the kids I baby-sit) swim in their pool for the first time of the season. Their mom had told me how excited they were to go swimming, and even though it would be cold, she didn't mind them splashing around in the pool.

So I bundled them up in their pants, long sleeve shirts, spring jackets, water shoes, and life jackets. What a sight! As for me, I sat beside the pool with my coat pulled tightly around me. This may have been peculiar and strange to some moms, but Sam and Katie's mom is very easy going. And the kids had a blast despite the temperature.

If I asked you what you thought was peculiar you might mention the boy in your history class with the spiked purple hair. Or the way your brother eats his lunch. Or your neighbor's extreme love for tattoos and body piercings. The Bible mentions the word peculiar seven times. And six of the seven times, it's referring to Christians.

The third definition for peculiar in the *American Heritage College Dictionary* (third edition) reads "belonging distinctively or primarily to one person, group, or kind: special or unique." God created us to be a special and unique nation for Him. We are His chosen people deemed to carry the gospel message around the world. I'm sure you've had many people look at you differently

Scriptures of the Day: Exodus 19:5, Deuteronomy 14:2, Titus 2:14, I Peter 2:9

because you're a Christian. But don't think of this as a bad thing. Be glad that God chose to make you a peculiar and special person in His eyes. So stand out, and jump into the pool of peculiarity!

Love poems come in a wide variety of forms—from the cutesy poem *"Roses are red. Violets are blue. Sugar is sweet, and so are you."* to Elizabeth Barrett Browning's well-acclaimed *Sonnet 43, "How do I love thee? Let me count the ways. I love thee to the depth and breadth and height My soul can reach."[15]*

Love poems have been used for hundreds (probably even thousands!) of years to express love to one another. There's just something about receiving a poem that makes the recipient happy. Who wouldn't be thrilled with a poem written specifically for them?

God has written a sixty-six book love "poem" to us. He loves us that much. To express your love for God, try writing Him a love poem. You don't have to write corny or sappy things, but be honest. Tell God why you love him. Praise Him for all He has done for you. Be proud that He is the love of your life. He deserves it. Jeremiah 31:3 says, "The Lord hath appeared of old unto me, saying, Yea, I have loved thee with an everlasting love: therefore with lovingkindness have I drawn thee." I John 3:1a says, "Behold, what manner of love the Father hath bestowed upon us, that we should be called the sons of God." God clearly expresses His love to us. Besides being commanded (Deuteronomy 6:5, Matthew 22:37), we should desire to show God how much we love Him too.

Everyone knows Romeo and Juliet's love story. Try to let everyone know about your love story with God. Let His love shine through you.

He hung on the cross. Naked. Mocked. Falsely accused. Hours earlier, one of His disciples had betrayed Him. His former followers yelled, "Crucify Him." A crown of thorns was jammed into His skull. He was spit upon. Beaten. Humiliated.

Yet in the last few moments of life, Jesus said, "Father, forgive them; for they know not what they do" (Luke 23:34).

Despite everything that was done to Him, Jesus still chose to forgive. What an example to follow! Many times, people hurt or wrong us, and we think, *Why should I forgive them?* Like times when someone cuts you off in traffic. Or makes fun of you in front of your crush. Or when the sales clerk is just plain rude. Or your little sister loses your favorite pair of earrings. During these times, it's very easy to get angry and throw a fit.

But think about Jesus and all the unfair things that happened to Him. Yet, He still forgave. So also should we. Matthew 18:21-22 says that we should forgive others "seventy times seven"—a short way of saying that we always need to forgive. Like Jesus.

So whether you need to tell your sister, mom, or friend that you forgive them, do it now. Make Jesus proud.

I've got a question for you. Take your time answering it because it's a very serious question. No, it's not question of life or death, but it is very important. First let me set the scene.

You and your boyfriend are standing on your front porch. It's dusk. The crickets are chirping peacefully in the background. Your boyfriend says he has something to give you. You eagerly wonder what it could be. After all, it's not your birthday or anniversary, at least not that you remember. Before another thought can cross your mind, you are handed a fully bloomed white rose. Even the thorns have been removed. To you, it's perfect! Smiling, you reach out and accept your gift.

Question… what would you have done if a wilted, browned rose strewn with thorns had been handed to you instead? I don't think you would have had the same reaction. I know I wouldn't! I'd probably throw the wilted rose back in his face!

So which rose would you prefer? Okay, I know the answer seems obvious, but to some people, it isn't so clear. Picture the white rose representing purity. On your wedding night, you'll be giving yourself entirely to your spouse. Which would you rather give your spouse a rose (or body) that hasn't been affected by sin's scars or a rose that has been soiled and used? If this helps, which would you rather receive?

I Corinthians 7:1b-2a says, "It is good for a man not

to touch a woman. Nevertheless, to avoid fornication." Because God has created man, He knows how our minds work. One touch never satisfies. God instructs us to guard ourselves by not touching one another in a way that would lead to lust or sin.

Of course, it is hard in a world centered on lust, sex, and greed to stay pure, but it is possible. If necessary, maybe you could only go on double dates or have someone in the room with you and your date at all times. But do whatever it takes! The best thing to do is pray for God's strength to help you fight the desires of the flesh. After all, with God's help, anything is possible. (Matthew 19:26) And with God's help, you will be able to hand your spouse a "beautiful white rose" on your wedding night and witness the joy it brings.

How well do you know your best friend? I mean really know him or her. Do you know their favorite flavor of ice cream? Favorite movie? Shoe size? Favorite car? Middle name? How about their mom's maiden name?

The more time you spend with someone, the more you learn about them. That's obvious. I couldn't tell you a thing about my next door neighbor, but I could answer every one of those questions about my best friend. Black cherry. *Frequency.* 10 1/2. BMW 23. Scott. Porr. Spending time with a best friend is always a priority. And a must. Talking to them three or four times a day is common. And a must.

But what about how much time you spend with God? He is the ultimate best friend! (Proverbs 18:24, John 15:13) He loves and cares for us more than any friend of ours. Yet, we usually don't desire to talk to God as much as we do our friends. We should desire to know who God is. The more time we spend with God, the more we get to know Him. And how awesome would it be to really know God? To know what He loves and what He hates.

In Proverbs 6:17-19, we see that God hates "a proud look, a lying tongue, and hands that shed innocent blood, an heart that deviseth wicked imaginations, feet that be swift in running to mischief, a false witness that speaketh lies, and he that soweth discord among brethren." In John 14:21, we see that God loves those who keep His commandments. By reading the Bible, we can find out a lot about God. Try it. After all, God knows everything about us. He loves us. And if we love Him, we should strive to do the same.

Following His Footsteps

Do you ever yearn for your childhood summer days? When you played outside until dark catching fireflies and romping around with your neighborhood friends. I'm sure you have many memories playing games like Mother, may I?; red light, green light; tag; and hide-and-seek.

One children's game we can still play today is follow the leader. God is our leader and guide for every one of our 896 questions, no matter the simplicity or complexity of them. He will guide our every step as we contemplate a confusing situation.

Psalm 37:23 says, "The steps of a good man are ordered by the Lord: and he delighted in his way." Every "step" or "way" in your life (Proverbs 3:5-6) is directed by God—if you follow Him. Sometimes though in follow the leader, you probably started to stray off the course from your friends. The same thing can happen in life. Something or someone will block your vision from God causing you to get off-track and maybe even fall. But just like God picked up the good man in Psalm 37:24 who fell, God will be ready to pick you back up too.

It's very important to keep your eyes on God as you travel along life's road. If you start to stray, have confidence that God will help you get back on the right path—if you ask Him. Now how about a game of follow the leader?

Scriptures of the Day: Joshua 14:8, Matthew 4:19, John 12:26

She described it as gray and bleak. The dirty cities left her speechless. Although some parts of Romania were wealthy, the majority of the country lived in poverty. For three months, my best friend Joni dedicated her time to help out in a Romanian girls' home. Girls from ages sixteen to twenty-two were pulled from orphanages and brought to the House of Hope to learn social and living skills as well as Bible lessons. I'm sure Joni had a lot of other personal matters that she could have been attending to, but she chose to give herself and her time to God.

God has provided us with so much—a comfortable home, a loving family, good health, and a mansion in Heaven to look forward to. And these are just the obvious blessings. But although God is generous in giving to us, we tend to be stingy in giving back to Him our time and talents. Instead of deciding to attend the Bible study or to pray for our missionaries, we choose to play that soccer game or to watch our favorite TV show. Soccer and TV are not wrong until they take away from God's time.

Hebrews 11:5 says that Enoch pleased God. Do you please God in your Christian life? Or do you make Him regret all that He has done for you? There are so many little things we can do to give of ourselves. We can write encouraging letters or send care packages to missionaries. We can offer to baby-sit the church kids so that their parents can go on church visits. Make a list right now of things you can do to make God pleased with your life. Give back to Him, as much as you can, while you still can. And the good news… you don't have to go all the way to Romania to do it.

Scriptures of the Day: Romans 8:32, I Timothy 6:17b

Every now and then it's crucial to stop and think of all the blessings in life—especially during the stormy times. Blessings fill our lives daily whether we're aware of it or not. I'll give you ten.

Hearing your favorite song on the radio

Hugs from your dad

Sunny skies

A smile from a boy

Compliments from friends

Hitting all green lights

A cozy bed

Funny jokes

An intriguing book

Test grade curves

This list could continue to fill up all the walls in your house.

Yesterday, my mom found out that she'll have to receive chemotherapy treatments for the rest of her life. Instead of dwelling on this awful news, she chose to dwell on the positive side of her situation—that her cancer tumors probably won't increase in size anymore.

Look for the bright side of a situation instead of dwelling on the negative. And remember, good can come out of bad. God has blessed you with so much. Make it a habit to look around you everyday for the blessings of life. Then you will always feel like you live a blessed life. Just like my mom.

Scriptures of the Day: Psalm 115:13-15, Psalm 126:2-3, Isaiah 12:4-6

I've often heard the question, "If you were on the witness stand for being a Christian, would there be enough evidence to convict you?" I don't know if you stopped to think about the answer to this question as much as I did. Sure, I live by standards and rules in my life, but that doesn't mean I'm a Christian. My friends know that I'm a Christian because they know me, but I wonder if a group of strangers could look at my life and conclude, "Yup, she's definitely a Christian." It kind of makes me wonder.

Through their testimony, Paul and Silas were able to lead the keeper of the prison to Jesus. All they had done was simply pray, sing, and obey the rules, yet this was enough to lead the jailer and his family to Christ. (Acts 16:25-34)

As Christians, we need to let Jesus shine through us so that we can lead others to the light of God's Word. If the world sees a wonderful change in us, they, too, would also desire this change. But if we're not acting any different from the rest of the world, they won't see the need to be saved.

It's like the "father who was teaching his son what a Christian should be like. When the lesson was over, the father got a stab he never forgot. The little boy asked, 'Dad, have I ever met one of these Christians?'"[16]

Let others know that you're a Christian. Invite them to church. Tell them you're praying for them. Show them God's love through you. And live your life to be pleasing to God. So others will be able to say, "Yup, she's definitely a Christian!"

Scriptures of the Day: Haggai 1:7, Romans 12:1-2

The other day, I read the following quote from Arnold Glasgow: "The key to everything is patience. You get the chicken by hatching the egg—not by smashing it."[17] Being patient—whether you're waiting for test results, the end of the school year, or for a big project to be done—isn't easy. But by being faithful, your hard work will pay off.

Galatians 6:9 encourages us to "not be weary in well doing." Hang tough when times are weary. Why? Because the end of the verse says, "for in due season we shall reap, if we faint not." We will receive the benefits of our labor. Just be patient, and keep fighting.

God has called each of us to do certain tasks. And through Him, we can accomplish great things. (I Thessalonians 5:24) When times are rough and the project is too hard, ask Jesus for strength. He will give it to you.

Think of Winnie the Pooh. He had great persistence and patience when trying to get honey from the beehives in the trees. Repeatedly, Pooh would get stung, stuck in the tree, or even fall from the tree. But he kept at it. And many times, he was rewarded with paws full of warm honey. If Pooh can remain faithful in obtaining honey, we can certainly remain faithful to God with the tasks and projects He has called us to do.

A person's last words tend to be meaningful. At least, the loved one at the dying person's bedside hopes that they will offer some truth or piece of advice for them to cling to.

Giving his sons one last bit of advice, restaurateur Fred Harvey said, "Don't cut the ham too thin." (His last words had to do with his job!) Financial editor and publisher Clarence Walker Barron's last words were of the same nature. He asked, "What is the news? Are there any messages?" On a brighter note, Charles Julius Guiteau, failed lawyer and religious zealot, remarked, "Glory, Hallelujah. I'm going to the Lordy. I come, ready, go!"[18]

Last words can be heartwarming or tear-jerking. It's amazing to see the difference between a Christian's last words and one who is lost. It makes me wonder what my last words will be? Would people know that I love God?

What's in your heart will eventually come out. (Proverbs 23:7a) You can learn a lot about someone from what they say. In Acts 7:60, Stephen, being stoned, requests of the Lord, "Lord, lay not this sin to their charge." With his dying breath, he asked God not to condemn those who had stoned him. What a testimony! He could have said so many other "choice words." But he didn't. His godly heart shone through.

When you're lying on your death bed, will your last words sound more like Stephen's or Fred Harvey's?

Scriptures of the Day: Proverbs 4:23, Luke 23:33-46

What are You Waiting for?

"A lone shipwreck survivor on an uninhabited island managed to build a rude hut in which he placed all that he had saved from his sinking ship. He prayed to God for deliverance, and anxiously watched the horizon each day to hail any passing ship.

"One day he was horrified to find his hut in flames. All that he had was gone. To the man's limited vision, it was the worst that could happen, and he cursed God. Yet the very next day a ship arrived.

"'We saw your smoke signal!' the captain told him."[19]

We can learn a lot from this story. Sometimes God answers our prayers, and we don't even realize it because it's not the way we would have expected. But God knows best.

Matthew 21:22 says, "And all things, whatsoever ye shall ask in prayer, believing, ye shall receive." All we have to do is ask and believe, and God will take care of the rest. George Muller knew this to be true. So did Elijah. (James 5:17) So did Peter. (Acts 12)

Pray for everything! Pray for your sister's cold to go away. For an "A" on your science test. For that boy to talk to you. For your future career. For a sunny day to have a picnic. Pray for everything on your heart. And while you're at it, pray for your friends. Ask them for a few specific requests that you can pray for. They'll greatly appreciate it. And the more things you pray for, the more answered requests you'll see everyday. God is waiting to answer our prayers. So what are you waiting for? Go Pray!

What makes you cry? Having your dad yell at you? Losing your favorite pair of pearl earrings? Getting sick on your sixteenth birthday? Spilling your glass of milk all over your Sunday dress?

I always cry Sunday night at 8 P.M. EST. I sit, cuddled in my chenille blanket with my apple pie candle burning, watching *Extreme Makeover: Home Edition*. And every Sunday night, no matter the family's story, I end up bawling. My husband is now familiar with my flowing tears. He no longer has to ask, "Baby, what's wrong?" He knows.

Did you know that the Bible tells us to weep when others weep? God wants us to comfort those who are hurting and try to share their pain with them. This loving act will encourage them, for now they will see that someone does honestly care for them. Especially with non Christians, this act can be a great testimony for Jesus' name. The aching soul will see God's love and peace shining through us as we help dry their every tear.

The good news in all of this is that we also get to rejoice with those who are rejoicing. When your friend receives tremendous news, get enthused for and with her. It'll mean more than you know. So can anyone join me next Sunday night at 8 p.m.? Don't forget your box of tissues!

It's extremely painful to say goodbye to your best friend whose dad just got a job transfer across the country. The tears will keep falling when you say goodbye to your beloved golden retriever because he's "too" old. It's hard to say goodbye to your older brother when he leaves for his freshman year of college five states away.

Since I have lived in Connecticut, North Carolina, Pennsylvania, Florida, and Ohio, I've had to say goodbye, adios, so long, farewell, toodles, ta-ta, hasta la vista, and shalom countless times to friends and family. The most recent goodbyes have been to my college friends. After growing inseparable through four years of college, the day came when we had to vocalize our farewells. We parted to our own home states of Massachusetts, Indiana, New York, Ohio, and Florida. And although we make it a priority to visit one another, the time always lurks when we must say our goodbyes at the end of each visit.

Through all of our goodbyes, there is Someone we will never have to say goodbye to. Our Lord is with us through each change and move that we make. And whether we move to Texas, Cancun, or Australia, we will never have to worry about leaving God behind. Every time you have to hug your friend, dog, or brother for the last time, God will be there waiting to give you the next hug.

What do the following items have in common: a glowing bride, a brilliant rainbow, a row of snow-capped mountains, a baby's first smile, and a person's feet?

The answer? They are all beautiful. I'm sure you agree with the first four items, but you're probably thinking that I'm crazy to call feet beautiful, especially if they're covered in warts and calluses. But it's simple. God says that they are beautiful.

Romans 10:15b says, "How beautiful are the feet of them that preach the gospel of peace, and bring glad tidings of good things!" We, too, can have beautiful feet, according to God's standards, if we are a witness for Him.

Share the good news of Jesus everywhere you go—from your neighbors to your hotel maid in Miami. The more people you witness to, the more beautiful your feet will become. And the nice thing is you won't have to spend any more of your hard earned money on another spa pedicure.

So get out there, and get some beautiful feet.

Dealing with Discouragement

I counted fifteen poison ivy blisters on my legs yesterday. I've blown my nose at least thirty-three times today. One of my best friends from college had to cancel his trip to visit my husband and me over Memorial Day weekend. The hairdresser messed up the highlights in my hair. I'm fighting to find the time to work, write, keep house, stay organized, and still feel connected to my husband, family, and friends.

But last night, I lost it. I lay on the floor and let the tears of frustration, hurt, and exhaustion flow. Today, I read the poem "I Refuse to be Discouraged" from an unknown author. Tucked in the back of my Bible, its pages are worn from being read so much.

But what a sweet comfort each word holds. My God is there to hold me up when I am weak. He's there to guide me when I've lost my way. He gives me such peace when I'm overcome with turmoil. He gives me quiet rest when I can't take another step. My God is my everything.

Although I may be discouraged and worn out, my Father's hand will guide me through every moment. And no matter how huge or trivial my problems may be, He still cares.

They're called stars, idols, and heroes. In reality, they're human. They make mistakes just like us. While watching *Entertainment Tonight*, the announcer said something like, "Next, we'll hear Jennifer Lopez's suggestions on how to make a marriage work." I had to laugh! She's already been divorced twice and is now working on her third relationship. Why would I take advice from her? You would think that the television producers could find a couple who have been married for twenty-five or fifty years and ask them for their advice. Instead, we hear from Jennifer Lopez because she's a "star."

Many times, what is popular is not always best. Just like taking marriage counsel from Jennifer Lopez is ridiculous, so is taking advice from a high school dropout about where to go to college. Or asking a drunk if it's all right to drink just one beer. Or asking someone who has "been around" if it's okay to have sex with your boyfriend.

In the above instances, it's obvious that we shouldn't ask for their advice. Yet many times we do, and we think it's okay. But it's not okay. We need to seek advice from those who are wise—like pastors, youth pastors, parents, and godly teachers and friends. These individuals can give us the kind of counsel we need to listen to. The kind that will help us make the right decisions.

Proverbs 12:5 says, "The thoughts of the righteous are right: but the counsels of the wicked are deceit." We need to be careful from whom we ask counsel. That's God's advice, and His advice is worth heeding. Not Jennifer Lopez's.

David had it when he fought Goliath. The lion in the Wizard of Oz wished for it. The firemen who gave their lives on 9/11 had it. Shadrach, Meshach, and Abednego had it when they didn't obey Nebuchadnezzar's decree. Give up?

In Deuteronomy 31:6, Moses tells the children of Israel to "Be strong and of a good courage, fear not, nor be afraid of them: for the Lord thy God, he it is that doth go with thee; he will not fail thee, nor forsake thee." A verse later, Moses told Joshua to be of good courage, for the Lord would be with him. Joshua and the children of Israel needed to hear these words. After all, they had to fight giants, win battles, and stay strong in the Lord. But these words can also apply to us. Even though we don't have to fight actual battles, we do have our own battles to endure. Battles of facing the future. Battles of saying "no" to alcohol and sex. Battles of nervousness before a big speech. Battles of having the courage to say hi to your crush.

We all have battles to fight. But God tells us to be of good courage. Psalm 27:14 says, "Wait on the Lord: be of good courage, and he shall strengthen thine heart: wait, I say, on the Lord." With God's strength, we can have the courage to fight our battles. God is 100% of our strength! (Exodus 15:2; Psalm 18:1) Lean on God when you don't think you can say no anymore and when you don't think you can give another speech for drama class. Be of good courage! God is there!

Have you ever asked God "why me?" I know I have plenty of times. Why is my car breaking down now? Why do I have to be sick during finals? Why do I feel so alone sometimes? Why does my mom have to have cancer? And the list goes on.

Many times, I've fallen on my knees before God, tears streaming down my face, pleading to know the reasons why I'm enduring my present difficulty. Until someone gave me this poem:

Resting in Him[20]
By Cornell K. Wilmoth

I do not understand, dear Lord,
Why this has come, nor see
Why days are dark and nights so long,
And clouds o'ershadow me.

Dost thou not understand, my child,
Why clouds o'ercast the sky?
That without rain no rainbow bright
Could be, and flow'rs would die?

So in thy life, my precious one,
Shall I send only sun
To wither, scorch what dormant lies;
And little raindrops shun?

Come lay thy weary head and rest
Upon my breast nor pine.
This is from me; I know what's best
Thy beauty to refine.

For I'll go with thee every step;
Thy pain and grief I'll share.
So lean harder, child of mine.
I've placed the burden there.

Every time I read this poem, it makes me realize that God is in control of everything that happens in my life. And through my trials, I'm able to learn more about God and the lessons He's teaching me through the pain. God is so good. He knows everything that we're going through. And through it all, He waits for us with open arms. We just have to lean on Him, and He will give us peace and rest through all of life's battles.

Wouldn't it be a thrill to win an all-expense paid vacation to Hawaii? Or Italy? Or even Florida? Everywhere you turn there are different contests, sweepstakes, and drawings trying to entice you to enter and win. Some even promise the reward of a dream vacation.

I wonder how the average American reacts when they get the telephone call informing them that they have just won. Many winners probably doubt the validity of the call. Some may think it's another prank call from cousin Earl. But the moment reality hits, I'm sure you could hear their excited screams from down the street. Or the next town, depending on the individual's vocal chords.

In reality though, you, too, have been rewarded with an all-expense paid trip to the most exquisite destination you could ever dream up. Here you'll be pampered with a street of gold to walk on, and every imaginable luscious fruit will be at your arm's reach for a snack. You'll live in a breathtaking mansion your entire stay. And the best part… this luxurious trip lasts forever.

God has prepared a home for us in Heaven. He created it out of His extreme love for us. And it's a free gift to those who have accepted Him as Savior. We'll never have to worry about paying rent or making mortgage payments on our mansion. God paid for it in full the day He shed His precious blood. What a priceless gift He offers to all those who ask. No drawings or sweepstakes involved.

Scriptures of the Day: Romans 3:24, Romans 6:23b, Revelation 21:16–22:5

In the 1998 movie *Sliding Doors,* Gwyneth Paltrow leads two separate lives. On her way home from being fired at her job, she just misses her subway car. From this point on, half of the movie portrays the life Gwyneth leads because she missed her subway car; the other half lets us peek into what life would have been like for her if she had caught the subway car. Throughout the movie, numerous different events occur in her life simply because she caught or missed the subway car. One simple act led to a chain reaction of events around her.

The same thing happens in our lives. Every decision we make and action we take affects those around us. You may think that cutting someone off in traffic is no biggie, but to the other person it may mean being too late to meet their long lost love at their meeting spot. You may think that having one beer at the party is okay, but it may cause your classmate to become a future alcoholic. By watching your example, your classmate may think it's okay to have a couple of beers with her friends. But she could get seriously addicted and not have enough willpower to stop.

As John Donne so wisely stated: "No man is an island."[21] As Christians and representatives of God, it is mandatory that we watch everything we say and do. We'll never know if someone is watching us from around the corner, or if our rushed actions lead someone else to sin. Ask God daily for control over your mouth and actions. Don't start a chain of events that you can't stop.

I can't remember who said it—one of the twenty-three or so Pre-K kids at the daycare I worked. I had asked, "How old do you think I am?"

Smiling, one child piped up, "You'd have to be seventy-eight!" I chuckled; so did they. At the time, I was only twenty-two.

A child sees things very differently than an adult does. To children, jumping in mud puddles is a great pastime. To an adult, mud puddles result in a huge mess and need to be avoided. To a child, watching a train pass at a rail-road crossing is an adventure. But to an adult, it's the extra few frustrating minutes that'll make him or her late.

More importantly, God sees things differently than an adult or child does. God's ways are perfect. When we compare ourselves with other Christians, we may think we're not so bad, maybe even better. But we have to remember that our view and God's view of sin are totally different. By following God's commands, we can learn to discern the right direction to take—away from sin. Fearing God is another step in learning how to view things from God's perspective. (Psalm 111:10)

So remember, the next time you're in a questionable situation, do not give in because "all your friends are doing it." Ask God to help you make the right decision. He will always be there to help. (James 1:5)

And hey, if you have to say no to a situation, why not go jump in some mud puddles instead? You'll be glad you did. So will your mom!

Marriage is truly the paradise of this world—if you marry the person God has designed for you. I heard countless marriage jokes, putdowns, and warnings before I got married (mostly from non Christians). It was disheartening, but I had such a peace that my Brian was God's will for my future husband. And since our wedding day ten months and twenty-two days ago, I have experienced a whole new love and respect for Brian.

Marriage can be wonderful if you're in God's will, have similar interests and views, and really know one another. I've always wondered how contestants on *The Bachelor* and *The Bachelorette* can actually chose one person for marriage. They hardly even get to know each other! I guess it's their way to find the right person. And as far as sharing the same views, I was reading excerpts online about marriage. One excerpt mentioned one of Ann Landers's most unusual stories that she ever received. It was from a husband who had hid his wife's dentures in order to keep her from voting for her Democratic choice. It really is helpful to have similar beliefs as your husband!

Yet the most important thing to look for in a husband is that he is a Christian. In II Corinthians 6:14a, the Bible says, "Be ye not unequally yoked together with unbelievers." This is a clear command for your future marriage. And although you may not think that you'll end up with your boyfriend Bill (who is not a Christian), you never can tell what the future holds. Like my youth director always

Scriptures of the Day: Amos 3:3, II Corinthians 6:14

stressed, "Every date is a potential mate." So be careful who you date. Make sure that they truly are a Christian. This choice will make all the difference in finding your paradise on earth.

I praise You for friends who hold my hand during my mom's battle with cancer.

I praise You for hot chicken noodle soup on a winter day.

I praise You for doctors, policeman, and firemen.

I praise You for the miracle of seasons.

I praise You for my new job.

I praise You for hugs.

I praise You for weddings.

I praise You for Rocky Road ice cream.

I praise You for the ability to learn a new language.

I praise You for a husband who loves to surprise me by doing the dishes.

I praise You for Christians who give their lives to be missionaries.

I praise You for homemade lemonade at Fourth of July picnics.

I praise You for a warm cozy bed to sleep in.

I praise You for slumber parties.

I praise You for summer.

I praise You for YOU.

Psalm 148:13
"Let them praise the name of the Lord:
for his name alone is excellent;
his glory is above the earth and heaven."

Do you drink? Do you smoke? Why not? Would you know how to answer these questions?

When asked if I drink, I would usually say something like, "I don't want to," or "I don't think it's right." I would again get the same reply. "Why?" This question stumped me. What reasons could I give my unsaved friends? Or my Christian friends? I grew up being taught that drinking is wrong. But why does the Bible say it's wrong? Besides my lighthearted answer that "it's just wrong," I knew I had to back my answer up.

I asked my dad if I could borrow a book about drinking. He gave me a book called *Alcohol: The Beloved Enemy* by Jack Van Impe. As I slowly flipped through each worn page, my beliefs grew stronger. The book steered me through passages in the Bible that explained why drinking is truly wrong.

Now I could show anyone who asks me why I don't drink verses like: Leviticus 10:9a, "Do not drink wine nor strong drink, thou, nor thy sons with thee, when ye go into the tabernacle of the congregation, lest ye die." And Proverbs 20:1, "Wine is a mocker, strong drink is raging: and whosoever is deceived thereby is not wise."

We all need to establish our own convictions. Colossians 2:7 says we need to be "[e]stablished in the faith." Secure your beliefs by digging deep into the Bible. That way you won't be wondering why you believe what you believe at a crucial time.

Yiddish folklore offers a telling tale about gossip-makers. One such man had told so many malicious untruths about the local rabbi that, overcome by remorse, he begged the rabbi to forgive him.

"And, Rabbi, tell me how I can make amends."

The rabbi sighed, "Take two pillows, go to the public square and there cut the pillows open. Wave them in the air. Then come back." The rumormonger quickly went home, got two pillows and a knife, hastened to the square, cut the pillows open, waved them in the air and hastened back to the rabbi's chambers.

"I did just what you said, Rabbi!"

"Good." The rabbi smiled. "Now, to realize how much harm is done by gossip, go back to the square..."

"And?"

"And collect all your feathers."[22]

This story is an excellent example of how impossible it would be to stop or change the gossip that is carelessly strewn around. Even though you may think that some new juicy tidbit of information is true, you must verify its accuracy with the source. False gossip can distort someone's identity. You wouldn't want people to think that you're a druggie just because their best friend reported to them that you were. You can't believe everything you hear, and you shouldn't spread everything you hear.

In Matthew 12:36, God says that we will give account of every word we speak. It kind of makes me wonder about what I've talked about the last five years of my life. Or the last ten. The good news is that today you can start fresh. Ask God to set a watch over your mouth. (Psalm 141:3) Let Him control what comes out. Not your friends.

"Holiday Inn, when looking for 500 people to fill positions for a new facility, interviewed 5,000 candidates. The hotel managers interviewing these people excluded all candidates who smiled fewer than four times during the interview. This applied to people competing for jobs in all categories."[23]

Although comical, this story is a good example. You wouldn't choose grumpy people to work at a very personable job. The manager's strategy revealed to him which people seemed happier. The same way they wouldn't have wanted grumpy people working for them, God doesn't want grumpy people "working" for Him.

It would be dreadful if the unsaved interviewed 5,000 Christians and only found 500 happy Christians. Being a Christian is the biggest joy in the world. We have a mansion in Heaven to look forward to. (John 14:2) A Savior who loved us so much, He sent His only Son to die for us. (John 3:16) And numerous other blessings and riches God showers down on us everyday. (I Timothy 6:17)

Don't let people look at your demeanor and think, *Man, I never want to be a Christian if that's how I'll look when I'm saved.* Let them see the joy that Jesus bestows so graciously upon you. Besides, it's not like you're on a job interview or anything.

Scriptures of the Day: Psalm 1, 33:12

Dear Jesus,

I'm tired. So tired. My heart is weary and heavy. There's so much going on right now, Jesus. I can't handle all the pressure. I can't. Jesus, please help me. Help me to get through this day, this hour, this minute. I have so much to do and so little time. I know this is the cry of many, but Jesus, I seriously can't handle any more stress. Everyday feels like a whirlwind, shoving me along its path. I don't even have the strength to go to classes today, let alone work tonight. Homework is piling up. I barely see my friends anymore. Not that it matters anyway, most of them don't seem to notice or care that I haven't been hanging out with them lately. O, Jesus, I'm so tired. I just want to curl up in Your arms and cry. I want You to hold me and tell me that everything is going to be okay. I need Your strength to get through this day.

Love, Me

Dear Child,

I know you are tired and worn. But I am your Strength. Look to Me, dear Child, I will help you through all of your trials. I'm watching over you right now, ready to help you whenever you ask. Lean on Me when your days are rough. I will give you the strength to endure all of life's battles. I love you, Child. Don't you see? I died on the cross for you, so that one day you would be able to live with Me in Glory. Just be patient, My Dear. Times will be rough. But I am always with you. I love you so much.

Love, Jesus

1. Insurance.It. 2006. http://www.insurance.lt/index.php/en/12779/

2. Hazel Felleman, ed. *The Best Loved Poems of the American People* (n.p.: Doubleday and Co., 1936).

3. Browne, H. Jackson. 2006. http://students.uwsp.edu/xvang231/soeportfolio/LONDON.HTM

4. Herbert V. Prochnow and Herbert Prochnow, Jr, *The Toastmaster's Treasure Chest* (New York: Harper and Row Publishers, 1979), 105.

5. Michael Hodgin, *1001 Humorous Illustrations for Public Speaking* (Grand Rapids, Mich.: Zondervan, 1994), 286.

6. Prochnow and Prochnow, Jr, 191.

7. Ibid., 93.

8. Hodgin, 355.

9. Lord David Cecil, ed. *The Oxford Book of Christian Verse* (n.p.: Granger, 1940), 164.

10. Gibran, Kahlil. 2006. http://www.kahlil.org/quotes60. html

11. Yarbrough Family Homepage. 2006. http://webpages. charter.net/kyarbrough/poemdidnthavetime.htm

12. Lehman, Frederick M. *Songs That Are Different*, vol. 2. 2006. http://www.cyberhymnal.org/htm/l/o/loveofgo.htm

13. Nystrom, Marty. 2006. http://www.pine-net.com/ ~obc/asthedeer.html

14. Mildred P. Harrington and Josephine H. Thomas, compilers, *Our Holidays in Poetry* (n.p.: The H.W. Wilson Co. 1929).

15. *Elizabeth Barrett Browning: Selected Poems* (New York: Gramercy Books, 1995), 148.

16. Hodgin, 60.

17. Glasgow, Arnold. 2006. http://www.inspire21.com/ site/ecards/key_patience.html

18. Ray Robinson, compiler, *Famous Last Words: Fond Farewells, Deathbed Diatribes and Exclamations upon Expiration* (New York: Workman Publishing, 2003), 41, 84, 99.

19. Michael Hodgin, *1001 More Humorous Illustrations for Public Speaking* (Grand Rapids, Mich.: Zondervan, 1998), 255.

20. Wilmoth, Cornell K. 2006. http://www.reallygood-news.co.uk/Resting%20in%20him.htm

21. Donne, John. 2006. http://isu.indstate.edu/ilnprof/ENG451/ISLAND/

22. Leo Rosten, *Hooray for Yiddish!: A Book about English* (New York: Simon and Schuster, 1982), 256.

23. *Bits & Pieces*, 3 March 1994, 11.

Beka DeWitt had the privilege of growing up in a Christian home, learning numerous lessons from Daniel and the big scary lions in children's church to the doctrine of soteriology in college. These lessons left an imprint on Beka's heart. Desiring to share Christ through the written word, she received her commercial writing degree from Pensacola Christian College in 2003. Since college, Beka has been busy working as a nanny, keeping involved in her church's ministries, and writing devotionals. In the fall of 2006, she and her husband Brian purchased their first home in Massillon, Ohio. In her leisure time, Beka enjoys spending time with friends, traveling, reading, and watching chick flicks.